THE HERB BASKET

An Illustrated Companion to Herbs

HAZEL EVANS
WITH GLORIA NICHOL

Satureja hortensis · Salvia officinalis · Rumex scutatus · Satureja hortensis · Rumex scutatus · Salvia officinalis · Rumex scutatus · Salvia officinalis · Satureja hortensis · Rumex scutatus · Satureja hortensis

Designed and created by
The Bridgewater Book Company
Written by Hazel Evans
Photography by Gloria Nichol
Designer: Jane Lanaway
Project editors: Veronica Sperling/Christine McFadden
Page Makeup Chris Lanaway
Step illustrations: Vana Haggerty
Border illustrations: Pauline Allen

4349 The Herb Basket
This edition published in 1999 by CLB
© 1996 CLB International
a division of Quadrillion Publishing Limited
Godalming Business Centre
Woolsack Way, Godalming
Surrey, GU7 1XW, UK
All rights reserved
Printed in Hong Kong
ISBN 1-85833-848-4

Mentha spicata · Calendula offici... ...anum majorana ·

THE
HERB BASKET

An Illustrated

Companion to Herbs

CLB

Calendula... ...officinalis · Mentha spicata · Origanum m... ...Origanum ma... ...majorana ·

CONTENTS

THE JOY OF HERBS

Marjoram

Mint

Marigold

RAGRANT, COLORFUL herbs are not only among the most enchanting plants in any garden but also the most useful. They appeal to all our senses, even that of touch, with their wide range of shapes and textures.

Herbs have come down to us through history, but over the years we have lost much of the valuable knowledge of how to prepare, preserve, and use them. Instead we have come to rely almost entirely on stores and markets for our food and drink, medicines, and beauty preparations. However, today, herbs are having a great revival, as people realize what a vital part they have to play in our lives. There is nothing difficult about growing and using these helpful plants. If you can grow garden flowers then aromatics follow easily. If you can follow a recipe then you'll have no problems about making a fragrant potpourri, putting it out in bowls to perfume a room. Added to your food or steeped in oils and vinegars, herbs bring sunshine indoors all winter long. And they offer so much more. They will scent your bath, soothe aching limbs, make calming teas to sip on a summer evening, and not only decorate your house but also keep insects at bay.

There is nothing more pleasant than to walk through your herb garden, however small it may be, at dusk on a summer's day, picking a leaf here and there, taking in the scents and perfumes, choosing what to use with a salad or a cooked dish. Even if you have no garden, you can still enjoy their company, for herbs will happily accommodate themselves on a windowsill, rewarding you not just with instant flavor for your food, but also scent and color. For herbs are not just our servants, they are also companionable plants – try for yourself and see. Discover exciting new ways that these unique plants can add flavor to your food, and fragrance to your home.

Grow several kinds of basil in the same container.

INTRODUCING BASIL

NE OF THE greatest of all the culinary herbs, basil is a plant of the sun. In France and Italy, you will find it on market stalls and on every housewife's windowsill as a first sign of spring.

Adopted by the Mediterranean countries since the 1500s thanks to the spice traders from the East, the food of Provence, Italy, and Greece would be unthinkable without it today. It was not always used in cooking. In ancient times, Galen claimed it was "not fitting to be taken inwardly."

Basil is also traditional in India where it is called *tulasi*. The Hindus grow it in and around their sacred temples, and it is laid on the breasts of their dead as a protection against evil:

> *Every good Hindu goes to his rest*
> *With a basil leaf on his breast*
> *This is his passport to paradise.*

The name comes from the ancient Greek, *basilikon phuton* meaning "royal herb," and in Greece today bus-drivers keep a sprig of it on the dashboard for luck. It was known in ancient Rome too, and is believed to have sprung up around Christ's tomb when his body was laid there. The Romans thought that the perfume of its aromatic leaves evoked love, and that a man who took a sprig of basil from a woman was her love for life. It was also thought to bring sorrow, recalling perhaps the legend of Isabella, immortalized by the poet Keats, who kept her lover's head in a pot of basil and watered it with her tears.

Basil has always had a powerful image. The herbalist Culpeper said that it "either makes enemies or gains lovers, but there is no in-between." Another herbalist, Parkinson, believed it bred scorpions under its leaves.

In Elizabethan England, basil was used as a protection against witches, and an infusion was taken as a cure for headaches. Today, the dried, powdered leaves are often prescribed as a snuff to clear the head.

Basil may be difficult to grow outdoors in colder parts of the country and at high altitudes. It loves the warmth and the sun, and is not happy in damp conditions.

9

INTRODUCING BAY

GROWN IN WESTERN EUROPE since the 16th century, the aromatic bay is said to originate from Asia Minor. A handsome evergreen, it has dark waxy leaves, attractive small yellow flowers, and dark purple berries in the fall. It takes well to clipping into shape. It seldom grows more than 26 feet tall and then only reaches that height in a sheltered spot. It grows particularly well in pots, which makes it a very decorative addition to a patio. Bay also comes in a golden version which is slightly less hardy.

The history of bay is inextricably linked to that of ancient Greece. It was dedicated to Apollo, and the oracles at Delphi, Apollo's temple, ate its leaves before giving out their prophecies. Bay has a mildly hallucinogenic property, which may be the reason they did this. The roof of the temple, too, was covered in bayleaves because the herb was believed to keep witches and lightning away.

In Roman times the famous bay wreath was awarded to victors, not just in athletics but in the arts as well. The word laureate comes from bay's Latin name *laurus nobilis*, and it has always been a symbol of wisdom and glory.

Bayleaves were used before holly to decorate houses and churches at Christmas time because of their alleged protective properties – Culpeper says that "neither witch nor devil, thunder nor lightning, will hurt a man in the place where a bay-tree is." He also believed that the berries were effective against "venomous creatures and the stings of wasps and bees."

Bay has always been considered to be a strong antiseptic and was used to protect people against the plague. An infusion of the leaves is said to aid digestion. A massage with its oil is also said to relieve rheumatic pains, sprains, and bruises.

BASIL, BAY, AND BORAGE

COOKING WITH HERBS

Always use fresh herbs if you can, to get the essential flavor. If you have to cook with dried leaves, halve the quantities of herb given in the recipe.

TIP

Add a bay - leaf to the water when poaching fish.

RIGHT: *Fresh bayleaves can be bought from specialist stores.*

11

INTRODUCING BORAGE

HE WORD BORAGE is believed to come from the Celtic word *borrach* meaning bravery. There is an old English saying "I, borage, bring always courage." A draught of the herb is said to have an exhilarating effect and for this reason an infusion of borage was given to the Crusaders before they set off to war. In earlier times it was the basis of a drink called "nepenthe," a wine that was said to bring absolute forgetfulness and which was given by the Queen of Egypt to Helen of Troy.

Borage is at home mainly in Mediterranean countries, where it grows wild and is known as bee-bread because it is much loved by bees. It is also called star flower, because of the shape of its brilliant blue flowers tinged with pink which are said to be the color of the Virgin Mary's robes. These distinctive small flowers have been featured throughout the centuries in needlework, and if you look carefully you will find them in many medieval tapestries.

Borage has always signified contentment. The ancient Roman writer Pliny claimed that it made one "happy and glad." Coles, the 17th century herbalist, said that it was "very cordiall and helpes to expell sadness and melancholy," for it was believed to revive and cheer hypochondriacs.

A poultice of borage leaves was used in medieval times to soothe swellings and sprains. In France today, an infusion is often taken for fevers and chest complaints. But its main claim to fame must be in classic cool drinks. In Shakespeare's time it was added to tankards of cider; today you will find it decorating the wine cup that signifies summer in England: Pimm's.

BASIL, BAY, AND BORAGE

PIMM'S NO.1

Makes 1
ice cubes
1 measure Pimm's
*3 measures clear
lemonade*
slice of lemon
sprig of borage

Put three or
four ice cubes in
a tall glass, pour
the Pimm's over
them, then the
lemonade, and
stir. Add a slice
of lemon, and
decorate with
freshly cut
borage.

FAR LEFT: *Borage
flowers are a beautiful
blue tinged with pink.*

LEFT: *Borage is difficult
to buy, so it's worth
growing your own.*

13

PLANT CARE

BASIL
Ocimum basilicum

Basil is a half-hardy annual. It grows up to 3 feet high, though dwarf varieties reach only half that size. It needs a sunny site but should be protected from the wind and from direct overhead sunshine that might scorch its leaves, so place it near a hedge or a wall. It prefers a light, well-drained soil, and hates heavy clay.

ABOVE *Basil can be grown easily from seed.*

Basil cannot be put out into the garden until all danger of frost is past, and it has to be sown afresh each year. The seeds are slow to germinate – the Greeks and Romans thought you should curse them as you sow them to make them sprout faster.

Start the plant off from seed by sowing it under cover in early spring, in a temperature of 55–60 degrees, using small pots or latticed "plug" trays. Avoid sowing it in open seed-boxes as the roots hate being disturbed.

Harden off the plants by moving them to a cooler place for a day or so before placing outdoors. Alternatively, you can sow them directly outdoors in late spring.

As the plant grows, pinch out the tops of flowering spikes to encourage them to bush out. Watch out for slugs and snails on young plants.

Water basil in the heat of the day; it should no longer be wet by the time the sun goes down.

Cut plants hard back in the fall and bring them indoors to prolong their season.

14

BAY
Laurus nobilis

This evergreen tree can grow up to 26 feet high. It is hardy in the South and Southwest, but you can lose a young tree in a hard winter. Bay likes plenty of sun, but prefers protection from the wind. It appreciates a rich, moist but well-drained soil.

Propagating bay is a long, slow process. Start it from seed by scattering the seed on the surface of barely moist soil in pots. Upend a clear plastic sandwich bag over each pot and secure with a rubber band to act as a mini-hothouse. It needs to be kept at 65 degrees. Germination is slow and inclined to be unreliable. Remove the covering once the shoots are 1 inch high.

Bay is raised professionally from cuttings in greenhouses where it can be misted constantly for a humid atmosphere. Raising it in pots under a plastic tent gives it the best chance of survival.

Grow bay from half-ripe cuttings taken in early fall, covering the pot with a plastic bag. Keep warm until fresh shoots appear, then remove the bag. Plant out the following year.

BORAGE
Borago officinalis

Borage is a hardy annual, growing up to 3 feet high. It likes a sunny, open position in the garden. It is a large, hairy, somewhat ungainly plant with gray-green leaves whose lax growth and untidy appearance is compensated for by its flowers. There is a white-flowered version too (*Borago officinalis* "Alba"), which is less often grown.

Grow borage in a light, well-drained soil that is not too rich. Choose a spacious patch because it will self-seed. Sow borage seeds 2 inches deep, in the open where the plants are to grow, in early spring. Thin the seedlings to 24 inches apart.

Remove flowers as they fade to encourage a fresh crop, and to avoid having too many seedlings. Dig up and discard plants that have finished flowering, as they will blacken and look unsightly after the first frosts.

The cut stems of borage are quite rough, so handle with care. Put them on the compost heap in the fall as they contain nitrogen.

PRESERVING HERBS

ASIL TAKES a long time to dry – rushing things will turn the leaves black. Cut, rather than strip, the leaves from the stem. Or leave them on the stems for the time being. If they have to be washed use tepid water. Spread the leaves to dry on cheesecloth over a wooden frame, making sure that they do not touch each other. Keep them away from light during the drying period at a temperature that does not rise above blood heat – by a heat source such as a radiator or furnace in the winter and on a shaded porch, or in a parked car left in a shady spot, on a dry summer's day. Once dried, the leaves should be packed in airtight containers.

Basil will freeze well. The easiest way is to paint both sides of the leaves with olive oil then put them in plastic sandwich bags, making sure that they do not touch, and excluding as much air as possible. Dry them flat in the freezer. Once frozen, they can be packed in layers. Be sure to keep dried basil in jars that are well away from the light, the leaves fade quickly in the sunshine and look pallid and unpalatable.

TIP
Cut your herbs from the garden a few at a time, and prepare them straight away. Wilted stems will not preserve well if you are planning to freeze them afterward.

LEFT: *Prepare herbs quickly and carefully for the freezer.*

BASIL, BAY, AND BORAGE

RIGHT: *Borage flowers freeze easily in cubes to add to summer drinks.*

Pick bayleaves off the tree and lay them out on trays in a warm, shady place. Avoid excessive heat and direct sun or they will lose their oils and fade. Dry them at a relatively low temperature and they will keep their attractive dark-green color.

When bayleaves are dried they tend to curl, so press them lightly between two boards for two weeks before packing them into airtight containers.

Bayleaves can also be dried in bundles for immediate use or made into a wreath which you "raid" from time to time. The best quality leaves will be those stored in jars. Bayleaves make welcome gifts for dedicated cooks, so look out for attractive jars in which to put them.

Borage leaves are difficult to dry as the plant is so succulent. They tend to turn black and lose their aroma if dried at too high a temperature. Dry them at low temperature in a well-ventilated room, on cake racks or wire mesh. Then crumble into airtight jars and store away from the light.

Preserve borage flowers in ice-cube trays. Place them facing upright in the sections, cover with water and freeze. Then tip the cubes out into plastic bags for the freezer. Drop them individually into cold drinks.

BASIL, BAY, AND BORAGE

GROWING A STANDARD BAY

MOP-HEADED bay trees, grown as standards in pots, can cost a great deal of money but are easy to raise if you have a little patience. Start off from a rooted cutting.

In the fall, cut or carefully tear off a straight woody shoot about 8 inches long with a heel on it (ie, a piece of stem). Strip off the lower sets of leaves that might be covered with soil when the cutting is inserted, then push one-third of the cutting into a 3-inch clay pot filled with a mixture of soil and sand, and firm it down well. Carefully water it from the top, and then firm it again.

Set your cutting in a shady place indoors – in a shed, a garage or on a cool shaded windowsill. Cover the whole pot with a large plastic bag, using a piece of twig to keep the "tent" away from the leaves. In spring, check the cutting by giving it a light tug. If it has rooted, take it out into full light.

Now transfer it into a 4-inch pot filled with potting compost to which you should add half a teaspoonful of superphosphate or slow-release fertilizer. Push a 24-inch bamboo stake down to the bottom of the pot alongside the stem, taking care not to touch the roots. Tie the bay cutting gently to it using raffia or knitting wool. Place the pot in a shaded place where it will have to reach for the light - this will make the stem grow longer and faster.

At this stage take off any side branches down the stem, one by one at weekly intervals, but leave any leaves as they help feed the plant.

Once the "trunk" of your cutting has reached the height you want it to be, pinch off the top growing tip. Now start taking off the lower leaves, leaving enough to bush out at the top.

As the side shoots grow, pinch out their growing tips to give you a bushy ball shape. Move the plant to a larger pot each time the roots outgrow their container - a warning sign is if the plant has a top-heavy look or has roots coming through the bottom.

TIP

Be sure to feed your topiary tree well, especially during its growing years. If you are starting with a bought-in plant, choose one that has one good straight stem, then transfer to a prepared pot and continue as above.

BASIL, BAY, AND BORAGE

1. Place your cutting on a cool, shady windowsill. Cover completely with a plastic tent supported with a twig to prevent it touching the leaves.

2. Re-pot in potting mixture with slow-release fertilizer. Stake and tie with twine or wool.

3. Pinch off the growing tip when the cutting has reached the required height. Remove the lower leaves to encourage the top to bush out.

4. Continue to pinch off the growing tips to achieve a ball-shaped topiary tree.

LEFT: *A full-grown topiary tree will last a lifetime.*

TIP
While your bay is being trained, be sure to feed it regularly.

PESTO AND PASTA

BASIL IS THE main ingredient of that classic
Italian dish, pasta with pesto sauce. Although
pesto sauce is best when freshly made, you can freeze it
successfully. Try it in other ways too, such as spooned
over split baked potatoes, as a pasta salad topping, or even
on French bread. If you make your own pasta, try using
chopped borage leaves as a stuffing for ravioli – a delicious
idea from southern Italy. Toss fresh basil leaves into pasta
shells too, to add last-minute flavor and color.

CLASSIC PESTO SAUCE

INGREDIENTS

Serves 4

2 cloves garlic
1/2 cup fresh basil leaves
4 tbs pine nuts (pignolas)
1/2 cup olive oil
1/2 tsp salt
1 1/4 cups grated Parmesan cheese

❖ Peel the garlic, and tear the basil leaves. Purée
all the ingredients, except the cheese, in a blender,
or crush them with a pestle and mortar, adding
the oil gradually. Stir in the cheese, then spoon
the sauce over hot pasta.

MARINADES

HE PUNGENT FLAVOR of bay makes it marvelous in marinades for meat dishes such as beef and pork, but it also goes unexpectedly well with fish. Bay also blends with strong spices such as chili and coriander (cilantro), giving added zip to their flavors. Thread bayleaves between slices of onion, beef, and tomato on kabob skewers to cook outdoors. Spear sea-fish such as red snapper with bay sprigs, or simply lay the sprigs on a barbecue and arrange pork or beef steaks on top.

CLASSIC MARINADE FOR BEEF

❖ To each bayleaf add a sprig of herb – any of the classics, such as thyme or marjoram, go well with bay – plus 1 cup dry red wine, ½ cup water and 2 tbs olive oil.

BOUQUET GARNI

HE TRADITIONAL bouquet garni is made from 2 sprigs of parsley, 1 sprig of thyme and a bayleaf, but try these variations:

FOR BEEF PROVENÇAL:
Bay with parsley, thyme, 2 cloves, and 2 teaspoons of grated orange rind.

FOR LEMON PORK:
Bay, parsley, thyme, and a strip of lemon rind.

TO MAKE A BOUQUET GARNI

❖ To make your bouquet garni, wrap the herb sprigs in a piece of leek leaf to make a small package, or tie together with  string or wool. If you include small items like garlic or cloves, place the ingredients in a square of cheesecloth, and tie with wool or string.

BORAGE FLOWER SYRUP

ERARD THE HERBALIST wrote: "A syrup made of the floures of borage comforteth the heart, purgeth melancholy and quieteth the lunaticke person." This syrup, which has a pretty, pale blue tint, is delicious poured over ice cream or with fruit compote or salad. Decorate the dish with fresh borage flowers.

INGREDIENTS

1 cup fresh borage flowers
boiling water
sugar

❧ Put one cupful of freshly picked borage flowers in a small bowl and cover with boiling water. Leave them overnight to steep.

❧ The next day, strain the liquid off the flowers into a pan, and bring to a boil. Pour the boiling liquid over another cupful of borage blooms, then leave to soak for 8–10 hours.

❧ Strain the liquid for a second time, pressing out all the juices from the flowers with the back of a wooden spoon.

❧ Measure the liquid, and add 1 cup sugar for each 1¼ cups water. Heat slowly until the sugar has dissolved, then boil the syrup fast until it thickens. Remove from the heat, skim, cool, and store in bottles or jars.

1. Put the freshly picked borage flowers into a small bowl and cover them with boiling water. Leave them to soak for as long as possible, preferably overnight.

2. Next day, strain off the liquid, boil it, and pour it over more blooms. Finally, strain it, and press the flowers through a sieve to extract all the liquid.

HERB TEAS

Herb teas are a delicious alternative to conventional tea and many have a medicinal value too – basil and bay teas both aid the digestion.

❧ Put a handful of herb leaves in a jug, pour 2½ cups boiling water over them, leave to infuse for a minute or so, then strain and serve.

OILS AND VINEGARS

HE BEST herb vinegars are made with the aid of the sun: simply fill a bottle with your chosen herb, pour vinegar over it, and leave the bottle on a sunny windowsill or porch for two weeks, turning it from time to time. Then bring it indoors, filter it, and re-bottle, adding a fresh sprig for decoration.

BAY VINEGAR

INGREDIENTS

Makes 2 ¹/₂ cups
bay leaves
2¹/₂ cups vinegar

Put the herb in a bowl then heat the vinegar to boiling point. Remove from the heat and pour it over the leaves.
Leave them to steep until the mixture cools, then strain, and bottle with a fresh bay sprig inside.

BASIL OIL

INGREDIENTS

Makes 1 cup
large handful basil leaves
1 cup olive oil

Roughly chop the basil leaves. Crush in a mortar, gradually adding enough of the oil to turn them into a paste.
Spoon into a bottle and add the rest of the oil.

Stand the bottle on a sunny windowsill, turning and shaking it from time to time. Strain and check the flavor. If it is not strong enough, repeat the process using fresh basil. Finally, transfer the oil to a sterilized bottle and add a sprig of basil for decoration.

BASIL, BAY, AND BORAGE

HERB OILS

*Basil leaves can
be perfectly
preserved in oil
to use later in
cooking. Fill a
wide-necked
bottle with
freshly picked
sprigs and cover
them with
sunflower oil to
preserve them.
Remove them
individually as
you want to use
them. Save the
oil to use in a
special salad
dressing.*

25

A CLASSIC BAY WREATH

TRADITIONAL bay wreath makes a wonderful decoration at Christmas – the Romans used it at their mid-winter festival of Saturnalia. It also looks good in the dining room or kitchen at any time of year. Set off its good-looking green leaves with red ribbons, red berries, rosehips, or red chilis, or decorate it, as we have done, with dried citrus slices. (These will take about two weeks to stiffen in a warm place.) If you can't get a vine wreath base, substitute one made from cane or a wire base covered with spaghnum moss or ribbon. Or make a frame out of crushed chicken wire and fill it with moss. Cut off strong, long leading shoots of a grape vine in the fall, and wind them into wreath shapes while they are still fresh and green. Bind the ends with wire or ribbon. Store them until you need them.

MATERIALS

Makes 1
vine wreath base
2 bunches raffia, ribbon or twine
branches of bayleaves
12 dried citrus slices
thread
glue

1. Cover the vine base with raffia or ribbon, winding it around until it is well covered.

THE CHRISTMAS WREATH

The Christmas tree is thought to have originated in Germany, and came to the U.S. with German immigrants in the 19th century. The wreath's origins are far older.

2. Pick shooting branches of bayleaves and cut them all to the same length – about 9 inches. Lash them to the frame by the base of the stem, using the raffia and making sure they all face in the same direction. Overlap them so that the base does not show. Tuck the last spray under the first one.

BASIL, BAY, AND BORAGE

3. Thread several citrus slices together and tie. Dot glue at intervals around the wreath on center leaves and stick the citrus slices to it.

TIP
You will find
the sprigs of bay
easier to use if you pick
them a day or two in
advance, then let them
dry off to enable them
to stiffen before
binding them to
the base.

27

A POTPOURRI WITH BORAGE AND BAY

AKE YOUR own potpourri to place around the house in decorative bowls, or in sachets for a lingerie drawer. In winter, put some in a pot and keep it by an open fire, or in the linen closet so that the warmth will release its delicious aroma.

RY THIS UNUSUAL spicy potpourri. Put it into bags for a handkerchief or sock drawer. Leave it in baskets topped with borage flowers. Get into the habit of saving orange and lemon rinds, and leaving them on a sunny windowsill to dry. They are a vital ingredient in many potpourris.

❖ Put the spices in a bowl with the orris root, add the essential oils, and combine thoroughly as though rubbing fat into flour.

❖ Mix together the dry ingredients, then stir in the spice mix. Place the potpourri in an airtight container. Store it for 6 weeks, shaking it from time to time, then decant into baskets, and top with borage flowers.

INGREDIENTS

½ tsp grated nutmeg
½ tsp crushed cloves
2 tbs dried ground orris root
3 drops lavender oil
2 drops oil of bay
1 drop rose geranium oil
1 cup dried lavender flowers
1 cup dried crumbled bayleaves
1 cup dried lemon verbena, lemon balm, or lemon thyme
½ cup dried camomile flowers
½ cup dried borage flowers
1 tsp shredded dried orange rind

TIP
Dry some extra borage flowers in silica gel to maintain their color and shape, and scatter them on the surface of the potpourri baskets.

A BORAGE FLOWER PINCUSHION

SINCE MEDIEVAL times, borage flowers have been depicted in needlepoint and embroideries. Make this pretty pincushion using the flower design below. You could make this embroidery on a larger scale if you prefer, still using the same chart.

It can also be turned into a small herbal cushion by using canvas and wool instead of the linen and stranded cotton. Increase the size of the stuffing, backing material, and trimming accordingly.

MATERIALS

5-inch square of 32-count craft linen
square of backing material the same size
stranded thread in blue, black, green, and pink
small ball of stuffing
strip of edging material 24 inches by 1¼ inches wide
24 inches of fine piping braid

❖ Fold the linen diagonally in both directions to find the center and mark it lightly with a pencil.
❖ Now taking the center as your guide, stitch the flower design in cross-stitch (see right) using 2 strands of thread at a time.

❖ Cut the fabric strip into 4 pieces. Turn under ¼ inch and press along one edge of each. Butt it up to the decorative stitching frame round the design and stitch in place by hand, cutting and mitering the corners so that the strips make a "frame" for the embroidery.
❖ Right sides together, sew the embroidered linen to the backing material, leaving a gap for the stuffing. Trim, press, and turn right side out.
❖ Stuff the pincushion, sew up the gap, then slip-stitch the braid piping around the cushion to cover the seam.

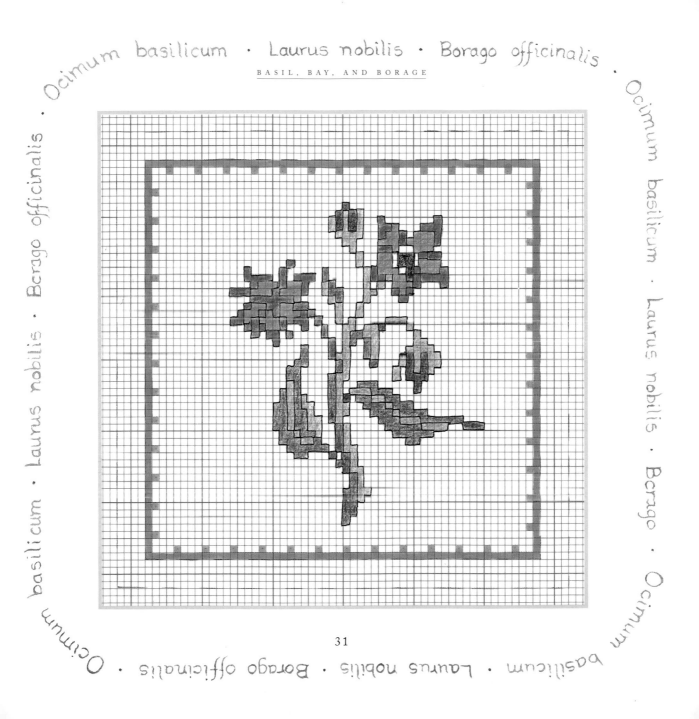

31

A lavender field
in England.

Lavandula officinalis · Levisticum officinale ·
Cymbopogon citratus · Lavandula officinalis · Levisticum officinale · Cymbopogon citratus ·

LAVENDER, LOVAGE, AND LEMONGRASS

INTRODUCING LAVENDER

LAVENDER is a shrubby plant indigenous to the mountains bordering the Mediterranean. It is believed to have been brought to England by the Romans. Although it has many other uses, lavender is usually associated with perfume. At one time England was famed for the world's finest lavender, but today the country has only one large lavender farm.

Now it is mainly grown and distilled in Provence in southern France, where in summer the landscape is laced with patches of bright purple, and, in the fall, plumes of purple smoke come from the distillery chimneys nearby.

Several types of lavender are used in the perfume industry. The best is the famous Super Bleue, with flowers of an almost violet hue, which comes from near Mont Ventoux in France. Super Bleue will only grow above 2,500 feet. It provides the basic essence for some of the world's most expensive scents and carries an Appellation d'Origine Contrôlée label, like fine wines.

LAVENDER

Lavender was one of the first herbs to be taken to America by the early settlers. "It is not for this climate" wrote settler John Josselyn in 1672. He was talking about growing it in Maine and northern New England, where it can be cut down in hard winters. Later, the Shakers, a religious sect founded in Manchester, England and who sailed to America in 1773, supported themselves by growing lavender, among other herbs, which they made into medicines and sold, thus starting the world's first pharmaceutical industry. The first Shaker catalogue listed 120 patent medicines for sale; among them was an extract of lavender that was prescribed for flatulence.

33

At the other end of the scale comes a paler variety called *lavandin*, which is used in more prosaic products – the flowers are used to make soap, kitchen, and bathroom products, while the stalks are used in thermal insulation.

Lavender is an ingredient in the once famous Four Thieves Vinegar, which protected French grave robbers from the plague. The herbalist Parkinson said that lavender is of "especiall good use for all griefes and paines of the head and brain." It was a tradition to wear a quilted cap stuffed with lavender to relieve headaches, and to this day a few drops of lavender oil smoothed on the temples do seem to relieve the pain.

Conserves of lavender used to be set on the table to flavor dishes and "comfort the stomach."

There are more than twenty different kinds of lavender, but the following are the most popular varieties:

COMMON LAVENDER
Lavandula angustifolia

Also known as *L. officinalis* and *L. spica* – called spikenard in ancient times, this is the most popular kind of lavender. It grows to a height of about 32 inches. Hidcote has dark blue flowers and slightly smaller leaves. It is a popular choice for low hedges, growing 18 inches high. Munstead is another short version that also reaches 18 inches. It has purple flowers on spikes that are shorter than other varieties and is also used for hedging, since it spreads rapidly. Twickel Purple, as its names suggests, has deep purple flowers. It grows about 20 inches high.

WHITE LAVENDER
Lavandula angustifolia "Alba"

Common lavender also comes in a white-flowered version that originates in the Alps, and a dwarf white lavender, Nana Alba, which does not grow taller than 12 inches and is good for low edgings around other herbs.

OLD ENGLISH LAVENDER
Lavandula x *intermedia*

This variety has lighter lavender flowers on longer spikes. The plant grows to approximately 24 inches high.

COMMON LAVENDER
Lavandula angustifolia

WHITE LAVENDER
*Lavandula angustifolia
"Alba"*

OLD ENGLISH LAVENDER
Lavandula x *intermedia*

FRENCH LAVENDER
Lavandula stoechas

WOOLY LAVENDER
Lavandula lanata

TOOTHED LAVENDER
Lavandula dentata

FRENCH LAVENDER
Lavandula stoechas

This is a pretty little shrub with narrow leaves and small violet flowers ending in tufts of brightly colored leaflets. This distinctive plant gets its name from the islands of Hyeres in the Mediterranean, which the Romans called Stoechades, where it grows freely. There is a another version called Papillon (*Lavandula stoechas pendunculata*), which has tufted "ears" on top of its blooms. It is not as hardy as other varieties.

WOOLLY LAVENDER
Lavandula lanata

This lavender has distinctive woolly leaves covered in silver-gray down and deep purple flowers on short spikes. It grows to about 20 inches high.

TOOTHED LAVENDER
Lavandula dentata

This has deeply serrated leaves and pale lavender-colored flowers. It comes from the south of Spain and may need some protection in winter, which is why it is often grown as a houseplant.

Lavandula officinalis · Levisticum officinale · Cymbopogon citratus · Lavandula officinalis · Levisticum officinale · Cymbopogon citratus · Lavandula officinalis · Levisticum officinale

LAVENDER, LOVAGE, AND LEMONGRASS

INTRODUCING LOVAGE

L OVAGE, ALSO KNOWN as love parsley or sea parsley, is one of the real old English herbs that used to be cultivated in cottage gardens all over England. It tastes like celery and in the past its stalks were often dug up and blanched, too. Lovage is sometimes grown as an ornamental plant in a herbaceous border and can reach up to 7 feet in height in lush conditions.

In some countries lovage is much prized as an aphrodisiac – in the Czech Republic, girls hang a sachet of leaves round their necks when meeting their lovers. The seeds are very pungent and the Greeks and Romans chewed them because they believed it aided digestion. Culpeper said that an infusion of lovage seeds "being dropped into the eyes takes away their redness or dimness."

Native Americans eat lovage raw, but peel the bitter outer stems before they do so. Because it has a very high vitamin C content, sailors used to eat it to avoid getting scurvy on long voyages. Once used in the treatment of rheumatism, the roots were also chewed by country people instead of tobacco.

FAR RIGHT: *Lovage's handsome foliage looks good in a border.*

BELOW: *Lovage makes an attractive foil to flowers.*

Lovage is widely used in France, Germany, and Italy in soups, casseroles, and stews. The stems can be candied, and they are often used as swizzle sticks for tomato-based drinks, such as Bloody Marys. The seeds, with their strong flavor, are used in Italy and in the U.S. in herb breads and cookies, or powdered and used like a pepper for seasoning. The unusual flavor of lovage – part celery, part yeast – is used commercially as the basis of some soup cubes. In the Middle East, its leaves are chopped into yogurt. In Italy, lovage leaves are put on slices of mozzarella cheese then marinated in olive oil. Lovage also has many uses in the home: the roots can be used to scent bath water and at the same time act as a deodorant, or to aid the circulation and make an invigorating herbal bubble bath.

LOVAGE

*Lovage comes under the astrological
sign of Taurus, the bull, the second sign of
the zodiac. It was used in herbal medicine in
medieval times for stomach disorders,
including colic, and as a gargle
for sore throats.*

LAVENDER, LOVAGE, AND LEMONGRASS

INTRODUCING LEMONGRASS

LEMONGRASS COMES from Southeast Asia. It is a coarse grass with a bulbous base that looks not unlike large chives, but feels woody and hard, has a strong smell and tastes of lemon. It needs to be grown in a high temperature, so it can be put outdoors in summer. It rarely or never bears any flowers and is grown from offsets rather than seeds. Its unique gingery-lemon flavor can be used in both sweet and savory dishes. It can also be infused in hot water as a refreshing drink.

OPPOSITE: *Try growing your own lemongrass – it's handy for oriental dishes.*

BELOW: *Lemongrass ready for harvesting.*

Lemongrass contains citral, an essential oil used in lemon flavorings. It is also used extensively to perfume soaps and colognes. Lemon oil is also used as a massage for stiff joints.

The roots and lower stem are used in oriental dishes in Ceylon, Thailand, Vietnam, and Southeast Asia. Lemongrass goes very well with fish, light meat dishes, and in sweet dishes – try infusing some in milk, then adding it to a rice pudding.

To release their volatile oils, the roots and lower stem need to be crushed or chopped before adding to a dish.

You can also find lemongrass in powder form. An infusion of crushed stems makes a lemon-

Lavandula officinalis · Levisticum officinale · Cymbopogon citratus · Lavandula officinalis · Levisticum officinale · Cymbopogon citratus · Lavandula officinalis · Cymbopogon citratus · Levisticum officinale

LAVENDER, LOVAGE, AND LEMONGRASS

LEMONGRASS
BOUQUET
GARNI

*The outer leaves
are used like a
bouquet garni –
put a bunch into
a slow cooking
dish, then
remove it just
before serving.*

flavored tisane that is very refreshing served poured over cracked ice cubes. It is also used in India, infused in milk, as a calming medicine for feverish patients.

Lemongrass is well worth growing for yourself to give a new and exciting taste to your cooking. It has another valuable property: in Thailand it is believed that having lemongrass in the house brings good luck to all members of the family.

TIP

If you have difficulty finding supplies of lemongrass, substitute slivers of lemon peel in marinades, curries, and casseroles. In salads use the chopped leaves of lemon balm, a hardy herb that is easy to grow in the garden.

PLANT CARE

N O HERB GARDEN should be considered complete without lavender and lovage. Apart from their many uses, they both have beautiful foliage – lavender's silvery needle-like leaves contrast beautifully with the glossy dark green stems of lovage. Coming from a tropical climate, lemongrass needs to be grown indoors, but its bamboo-like shoots look good on a kitchen windowsill.

To grow lavender from cuttings, put several in one pot. To speed up rooting, put wire hoops over them and cover with a "tent" made out of a clear plastic sandwich bag.

LAVENDER
Lavandula

A hardy evergreen shrub (but *stoechas* and *lanata* are tender varieties). It can grow up to 4 feet but there are many compact varieties available. Lavender prefers sunshine and likes a light, well-drained soil that is not too rich. Put lavender plants 2 feet apart. Sow lavender seeds on the surface of the soil in a seed tray in the fall and give them some bottom heat if you can. Transfer the seedlings into pots containing well-drained compost; keep them in a cold greenhouse or cold frame until the spring. Let the roots get well established before you put them in the ground.

Lavender roots very easily. Take ripe cuttings in the fall, setting several into a pot. Leave young plants indoors to overwinter.

Lavender should be cut back hard in the spring and trimmed after flowering.

LAVENDER, LOVAGE, AND LEMONGRASS

LOVAGE
Levisticum officinale

This hardy perennial can grow up to 6 feet in height. It can take partial shade and thrives in a moist fertile soil, but its roots should be protected in severe winters. Set your lovage plants 2 feet apart. Keep them well watered for fresh supplies of foliage.

Sow seeds outdoors in the fall and thin out in the spring. Take off the flowers as they appear to allow the roots to swell if you are using them for cooking. But allow some plants to flower in order to save the seeds.

Divide the clumps in the autumn and remove the large outside leaves.

SPLITTING A LOVAGE PLANT

When it has formed a large clump, lovage can be divided. Simply plunge two small hand forks, back to back, into the center of the plant and pull them apart. If the clump is very large and the roots tough, you could chop it in half with a spade.

LEMONGRASS
Cymbopogon citratus

This perennial tropical grass grows like bamboo and achieves a height of up to 6 feet in tropical conditions, but no more than 3 feet in a container.

Lemongrass is normally grown from offsets planted in the spring.

The easiest way to raise your own is to buy some fresh lemongrass from an ethnic grocer or supermarket and put it in water, where it should sprout roots.

Lemongrass needs a temperature above 56 degrees at all times. It prefers a rich water-retentive soil (avoid lightweight composts) and needs constant moisture – mist it frequently and divide large clumps in the fall.

HOW TO PROPAGATE LEMONGRASS

You can raise your own with lemongrass bought from a shop, but make sure it is green and fresh-looking. Suspend a bundle in water until it sprouts whiskery roots, then transfer to pots.

PRESERVING

AVENDER DRIES VERY easily. Tie the spikes into bunches and hang them upside down in a warm, dark place. The process normally takes about fourteen days. To speed things up you can dry the stems individually on cake racks, or in small bunches of five or six spikes at a time poked through holes in a chicken wire frame.

Under wraps, lavender flowers will keep their fragrance for up to five years. The best way to store them is in paper bags. The actual flowers have no fragrance – it is the tiny green bracts at their base that give off the aroma.

To dry lavender leaves for potpourris, sachets and bath bags, hang up the stems for five days to harden them a little, then strip off the leaves into paper bags and store in an open, well-ventilated place.

RIGHT: *Lavender, lovage, and lemongrass all preserve well.*

Tie stems of lovage together and hang them up to dry or lay them out on wire racks. The leaves, which have the most flavor, will dry before the stems. Crumble them on to a sheet of paper, then decant them into glass jars. Lovage leaves can also be frozen successfully in small plastic bags.

Lavandula officinalis · Levisticum officinale · Cymbopogon citratus · Lavandula officinalis · Levisticum officinale · Cymbopogon citratus · Lavandula officinalis · Levisticum officinale · Cymbopogon citratus

LAVENDER, LOVAGE, AND LEMONGRASS

LEMONGRASS

This herb comes under the earth sign of Capricorn, and has the protection of the Dragon in ancient oriental astrology.

The young green tips of lemongrass can be put into plastic sandwich bags and then frozen. Flatten the bag with the palm of your hand to expel as much air as possible. Alternatively they can be frozen in little parcels made up from aluminum foil.

The whole plant can be dried, then crumbled. This is best done in a low oven with the door open, or in a linen closet, which is a longer process. Split the stems lengthwise and spread them on wax paper on a plate or a board. They will take at least two weeks to dry. They can eventually be crumbled and put into jars. Store them in a cool, dark place and use within six months.

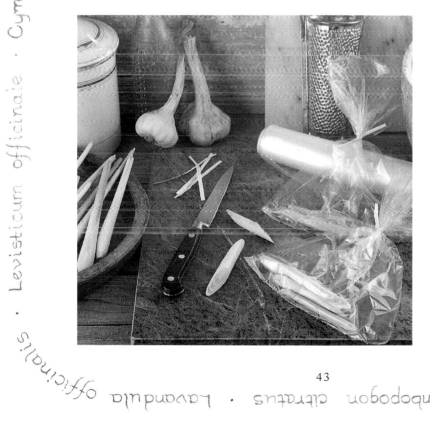

LEFT: *The easiest way to preserve lemongrass is to freeze it in plastic bags. Dried lemongrass can be used in place of fresh leaves in cooking, but the flavor will be much more pungent, so quantities should be reduced.*

43

PLANTING A LAVENDER HEDGE

HERBAL HEDGE not only makes an aromatic edge to a herb garden, but looks good around a flower border, too. The quickest and easiest way of creating a lavender hedge is to make one from container-grown cuttings which you have taken yourself or bought from a nursery.

TIP

Water your hedging plants well in the first few weeks. Remember, when they are fully grown they will need watering in periods of drought, as the thick bushy growth will stop moisture reaching the roots.

1. Use a length of twine and two pegs to mark a straight line, or a length of hose to make a curve, and make a row of holes where your plants are to go. Sprinkle a little organic fertilizer in and around the site.

2. Working as quickly as possible so that the roots are not exposed to the elements, set your plants into the ground. Full-size lavenders should be set 24 inches apart, smaller varieties like Munstead about 12 inches apart.

3. Clip the tops regularly to encourage side growth. Once the hedge is established, cut it back severely each spring, and, as it grows, trim it so that the sides slope a little and the base is broader than the top.

LAVENDER, LOVAGE, AND LEMONGRASS

Lavender looks good in a border.

HERB OILS

OTH LOVAGE and lemongrass can be used to make delicious herb oils. Use them in cooking – fry meat or spices in lemongrass oil, use lovage oil to sweat the onions for a soup and to make unusual salad dressings. When making these herb oils it is best to use a bland base, such as peanut or sunflower, rather than olive oil, as its taste would be too intrusive.

LOVAGE OIL

INGREDIENTS

Makes 2 cups
bunch of fresh young lovage leaves
2 cups sunflower oil

❖ Crush the leaves with a mortar and pestle, add a little of the oil and crush them again. Continue until half the oil is used, then transfer the mix to a bottle. Add the remaining oil and shake. If you do not have a mortar and pestle you can use a food processor, but only blend very briefly (for the count of five) or the oil will become hazy.

❖ Leave the bottle on a sunny windowsill or in a warm place, giving it a shake from time to time. After two weeks, strain the oil through muslin, pour it into a fresh bottle and add a sprig of fresh lovage for decoration.

LEMONGRASS OIL

INGREDIENTS

Makes 2 cups
handful of lemongrass stalks
2 cups sunflower oil

❖ Lay the lemongrass stalks on a wooden board and crush them lightly with a hammer wrapped in a piece of muslin. It is essential to bruise the stalks this way in order to extract the essential oils.

❖ Place them in a wide-necked bottle, warm the oil to blood heat and carefully pour over the lemongrass.

❖ Leave the mix for at least one month in a warm place, shaking the bottle from time to time.

❖ Pour off the oil through muslin into a fresh bottle, add a slice of lemon for decoration and seal tightly.

LAVENDER, LOVAGE, AND LEMONGRASS

LAVENDER, LOVAGE, AND LEMONGRASS

A DRIED LAVENDER SHEAF

SHEAVES OF DRIED lavender look very chic, but cost a great deal. Here's how to make one for yourself at a fraction of the price. Harvest the lavender when it is at its best – when the flowers are just about to bloom.

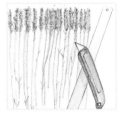

1. Lay the lavender spikes on a board, matching up their tips so that they are exactly in line with each other.

2. Measure the length of the stalks by placing your chosen container a suitable distance from the tips. Then trim the base of the stalks. Secure with a rubber band. Stand somewhere warm and well ventilated to dry, out of direct light.

3. When the lavender is completely dry, wrap the middle of the spikes with a piece of florist's wire, taking care it does not cut into the stems. Push the stems into a pot containing moss.

TIP
If you leave the harvested lavender spikes to dry and harden for a day or two before using, they are easier to handle.

LAVENDER, LOVAGE, AND LEMONGRASS

AROMATIC MATS

IT'S PLEASANT to smell the aroma of lemon or lavender as you set a hot pan or teapot down on the kitchen table. And it's easy to achieve with these pretty quilted place mats stuffed with fragrant dried lavender or lemongrass.

They make welcome gifts. Collect attractive fabric remnants to make them with, choosing a plain or contrasting patterned fabric for the backing.

MATERIALS
Makes 1
square of decorative fabric 10 × 10 inches
square of backing fabric (felt or plain cotton)
the same size
square of thin wadding the same size
good handful of dried lavender or lemongrass
length of bias binding 30 inches long
some dressmaking chalk

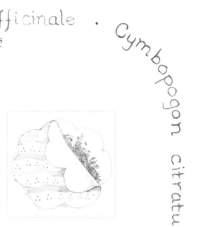

1. *Cut out the scalloped shape in the top fabric, backing fabric and wadding. Seam them together, leaving a space for the stuffing. Draw on guidelines for quilting in chalk on one side.*

2. *Stuff with dried lavender or dried lemongrass. Seam up the gap by hand.*

3. *Keeping it flat so the stuffing does not shift, quilt the mat carefully by hand or machine along the chalk lines.*

4. *Pin then stitch the bias binding to the edges of the front of the mat.*

LAVENDER, LOVAGE, AND LEMONGRASS

Lavandula officinalis · Cymbopogon citratus · Levisticum officinale · Cymbopogon citratus · Lavandula officinalis · Levisticum officinale

Lavandula officinalis · Levisticum officinale · Cymbopogon citratus · Lavandula officinalis · Levisticum officinale · Lavandula officinalis · Cymbopogon citratus · Levisticum officinale

LAVENDER, LOVAGE, AND LEMONGRASS

HERBAL BUBBLE BATH

OTH LAVENDER and lemongrass can be used to make your own bubble bath and toilet waters – lavender to stimulate the skin, lemongrass to soothe it. Substitute or add other herbs, too, to make your own personal versions. Start collecting decorative antique glass bottles in which to keep your bath and toilet waters.

INGREDIENTS

Makes 2¹⁄₂ cups

1¹⁄₄ cups top quality unperfumed dishwashing liquid

1¹⁄₄ cups distilled water

4 drops essential oil of lavender or lemongrass

2 drops blue or yellow food coloring (optional)

1. *Pour the ingredients into a 2¹⁄₂ cup container and shake thoroughly, then put into a decorative bath bottle.*

PERFUME

The word perfume comes from the Latin per fume *– "through fire." The first scents were the aromatic woods burned in their temples.*

LAVENDER WATER

SE LAVENDER water to give a delicious scent to a bath, or as a personal perfume. Keep a bottle in the fridge in summer so that you can dip a handkerchief into it to cool your brow.

INGREDIENTS

Makes 2²⁄₃ cups

2¹⁄₂ cups distilled water

¹⁄₄ cup vodka

8 drops essential oil of lavender

1. *Shake the ingredients together thoroughly in a container, then decant into decorative bottles.*

Marjoram comes in several decorative guises.

INTRODUCING MARJORAM

MARJORAM IS one of the oldest herbs that is in general use today. A native plant of the Mediterranean region, the Greeks gave it its name *oros* and *ganos* which means "joy of the mountains." It was said to have been created by Aphrodite, the goddess of love, whose touch gave marjoram its sweet spicy perfume. Not surprisingly, Greek couples often wore crowns of marjoram when they married, and wreaths of marjoram were laid on the dead to ensure they went to a happy life in the next world. Another myth claims that the King of Cyprus punished a servant for dropping a jar of perfume by turning him into a marjoram plant.

In ancient Egypt, marjoram was used as a disinfectant and to help preserve mummies in their tombs, but it was the Romans who spread its use all over Europe.

Marjoram was described by Shakespeare as a "herb of grace." It was one of the many herbs used to protect people from the plague. Sweet marjoram was used in Tudor times as an edging for knot gardens, and its oil was used to polish furniture and floors. Marjoram oil is much prized in some countries to rub on aching rheumatic joints, to cure toothache, and soothe morning sickness. Aromatherapists use the essential oil for a relaxing massage.

There is not just one, but a whole family of marjorams. All of them have the same spicy, slightly sweet taste, but of a varying intensity, according to which part of Europe, North Africa, or America they come from. It is the sun, or absence of it, that makes a great deal of difference to the pungency of marjoram's flavor.

There are many strange myths about marjoram. Gerard, the herbalist, said that a herb tea of marjoram would benefit those who "are given to overmuch sighing." Portuguese children believe to this day that if you sniff marjoram your nose will drop off. Tortoises are said to chew it to fortify themselves before a fight. Back in ancient times, Aristotle remarked that these curious creatures used it as an antidote to poisoning.

INTRODUCING MINT

MINT HAS been held in high esteem throughout the centuries, being much prized in the Middle East and especially in North Africa, where it is used extensively for mint tea. The name comes from the beautiful nymph, Minta, who was pursued by Hades, the god of the underworld. His jealous wife, Persephone, cursed the maiden and turned her into a plant destined to live in the shade – a place that mint prefers to this day. For this reason it makes good ground cover in shady places.

People in countries such as India have hung it in their doorways for centuries to give the impression of coolness in a hot climate. Mint contains menthol, which gives the skin a sensation of coolness. It has long been used as a panacea for digestive problems, and in the 17th century Dr Andrew Borde, author of *Regyment of Helth,* suggested using it as a remedy for "sighynge and sobbynge."

The common mint that appears in most of our gardens is only one of a whole family of

ABOVE: *There are a multitude of different mints from which to choose.*

eighteen or more different varieties ranging from Corsican mint, with tiny leaves and prostrate habit, to the so-called Irish mint (*Mentha raripila rubra*) which has dark, red-tinged leaves and actually makes a red mint sauce. There is even a water mint (*Mentha aquatica*) which thrives in marshy conditions and has the same strong flavor as the others. The variegated versions of mint, like *Mentha gentilis,* are decorative plants in their own right in any flowerbed.

MARJORAM, MINT, AND MARIGOLD

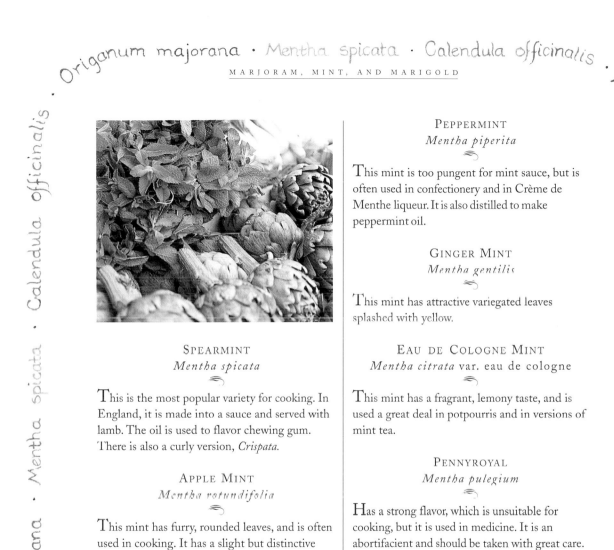

SPEARMINT
Mentha spicata

This is the most popular variety for cooking. In England, it is made into a sauce and served with lamb. The oil is used to flavor chewing gum. There is also a curly version, *Crispata*.

APPLE MINT
Mentha rotundifolia

This mint has furry, rounded leaves, and is often used in cooking. It has a slight but distinctive flavor of apple, hence its name. "Bowles Mint" (*M. rotundifolia* var. Bowles) has a particularly good flavor for mint sauce and is not as subject to the rust disease as other mints.

PEPPERMINT
Mentha piperita

This mint is too pungent for mint sauce, but is often used in confectionery and in Crème de Menthe liqueur. It is also distilled to make peppermint oil.

GINGER MINT
Mentha gentilis

This mint has attractive variegated leaves splashed with yellow.

EAU DE COLOGNE MINT
Mentha citrata var. eau de cologne

This mint has a fragrant, lemony taste, and is used a great deal in potpourris and in versions of mint tea.

PENNYROYAL
Mentha pulegium

Has a strong flavor, which is unsuitable for cooking, but it is used in medicine. It is an abortifacient and should be taken with great care. Grow pennyroyal for decoration, not for the table.

ABOVE: *Look out for mint at farmers' markets.*

The true marigold has deep orange flowers.

INTRODUCING MARIGOLD

ARIGOLD IS a flower of the sun. It came from India (where it is traditionally used to crown the statues of Hindu gods and to decorate their temples), and from Persia where it was first used in food. It reached this country via southern Europe, but takes happily to our climate. Its official name, calendula, comes from the Latin *calend*, meaning calendar, because it was believed to flower on the first day of every month. Indeed, it flowers almost all year round in warm climates.

The "pot marigold," as the true marigold is sometimes called, is much appreciated as a herb as well as a flower. It has been used in household dyes, in butters, and to give a rich tone to casseroles and stews. But it has healing and antiseptic properties, too. In the American Civil War wounds were treated with marigold leaves, and in the First World War, when medicines became in short supply, a paste of calendula was used on the wounds of soldiers. The sap of marigold is also said to soothe bee and wasp stings. The ancient Egyptians believed it would rejuvenate the skin, and it has been rediscovered today and used in many ranges of natural cosmetics.

Marigold has always been a flower of love and was used in magic spells to bewitch people.

Early herbals say that just looking at marigold will "drive evil humour out of the head." Gerard the herbalist noted that it was used in "Dutchland against Winter for broths and Physicall potions." Its bright petals are called "poor man's saffron" with good reason for they impart a yellow coloring to food when cooked.

If you are growing it for flavor be sure to get the true marigold – *Calendula*, rather than the African or French hybrids – *Tagetes*.

MARJORAM, MINT, AND MARIGOLD

PLANT CARE

*Clip pot –
grown mints
and marjorams
frequently to
keep them
bushy.*

MARJORAM
Origanum

This herb grows to a height of up to 12 inches depending on the variety. It needs a sunny situation and a well-drained soil, preferring one that is alkaline (chalky). It tends to become woody at the base with leggy shoots, so it should be trimmed back from time to time and some of the dead wood cut away. Divide over-large clumps, since if it becomes tough and overgrown its flavor tends to deteriorate. Pull off some pieces of root in the fall, pot them, and bring them indoors to grow under cover and give you winter greenery.

MINT
Mentha

A perennial plant which grows up to 2 feet high from creeping roots which spread very rapidly and, if you are not careful, can soon take over a corner of the garden. Mint will grow almost anywhere in the garden and enjoys the shade. If you are short of space, it is best to plant it in a bottomless bucket sunk in the ground. Mint is best grown from pieces of root or cuttings, as it does not always come true to form if you start it from seed. Snip the plants frequently, and pinch out the flowers to keep the plants bushy and encourage plenty of young growth which is what you need. Bring one or two roots indoors and grow the plant in pots to give you supplies of fresh mint in mid-winter.

1. To keep mint from encroaching on the plants around it, take the bottom out of a tin or bucket, sink it in the ground, then plant the mint in the center.

MARIGOLD
Calendula officinalis

Marigold is a hardy annual, grown each year from seed and reaching a height of up to 24 inches. It prefers the sun and will grow in almost any soil as long as it is not waterlogged. Sow marigold in the spring in a sunny place and thin the seedlings out to 10 inches apart. Or start it off in pots in the fall or sow it, one seed at a time, in divided seedtrays, transferring the seedlings to pots later. Once fully established, marigold will go on to seed itself from year to year.

1. To sow marigolds put several seeds in a pot, and cover them with potting mixture. Keep the soil moist at all times.

2. When the seedlings are large enough to handle, transfer them carefully into individual pots.

Mint and marjoram hanging up to dry.

DRYING YOUR HERBS

HEN DRYING herbs make sure that this is done as quickly as possible. Choose somewhere that has a good flow of air to get rid of moisture as speedily as you can. Once dry, the herbs should be stored immediately in a dark place. Avoid any contact with moisture as the herbs will re-absorb it and become musty.

Hang marigold flowers up by their stems to dry, suspending them from a rack or fine chicken wire so that they do not touch each other.

Spread marigold petals on paper, spacing them out in a warm, dark place. As soon as they are crisp and dry, put them in opaque jars or airtight containers. If they are in clear jars, they should be stored away from the light or they will lose their color.

Keep harvested marigold seed in paper bags or envelopes ready for re-sowing.

Mint can be dried in bunches, hung in a warm, dark place. Do not leave it too long – the moment that the leaves turn crisp, crumble them onto a sheet of paper, then store them in jars or airtight containers. The leaves can also be frozen very successfully in plastic sandwich bags. Or you can mince them, ready for cooking and drinks, and freeze in sections in an icetray. Decant the cubes when they are frozen and store them in a bag in the freezer.

Marjoram can be dried in bunches but is best done sprig by sprig, laid out on paper on a wire rack. If you dry them in bunches, once the leaves are crisp, plunge the bunch into a paper bag and strip off the leaves.

Marjoram can also be frozen, but releases its flavor best by being preserved in oil or vinegar.

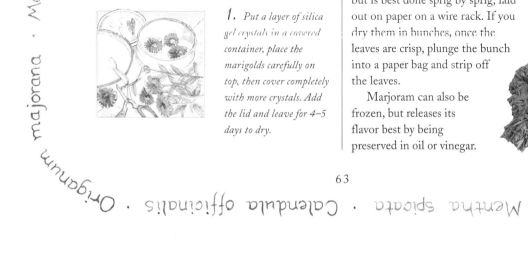

1. Put a layer of silica gel crystals in a covered container, place the marigolds carefully on top, then cover completely with more crystals. Add the lid and leave for 4–5 days to dry.

A HERBAL ROCK GARDEN

HERB ROCKERY makes a marvelous way to show off smaller, shrubbier plants, such as marjoram. So if you already have a rock garden, consider converting it to aromatics. You'll find that the prostrate varieties work well.

A garden like this is ideal for Mediterranean plants like thyme, marjoram, and sage, which will knit together to make a carpet of color. The rocks will shelter shade-loving plants and also help to keep the roots of stronger growers like mint under control. Choose prostrate versions of plants as much as possible – dittany of Crete (*Origanum dictamnus*) looks particularly good in a rockery setting and so does golden marjoram. And tiny creeping mints, like pennyroyal and Corsican mint, will give a contrasting dark green color.

1. Start by making a mound of soil. Dig in plenty of good compost or add fertilizer. Make the mound rounded rather than sharp. If you are short of stones, try making a rockery in a corner which can be very effective.
Push your rocks well in place in the soil.

2. Using a trowel, put your plants in place then scatter gravel evenly over the surface.

A MINI-LAWN

Make a miniature lawn on the top of a rocky outcrop, using Corsican mint. Given the minimum of soil it will form an attractive tiny green carpet.

A KITCHEN PLANTER

ROW HERBS in the kitchen, too. Provided you have a sunny window they are certain to thrive. Bring pieces of plant in at the end of the summer and they will go on growing for you through the winter. Marigolds will continue to flower, basil will thrive, and you'll have supplies of fresh marjoram and mint to cut at Christmas time.

One of the most attractive types of container for herbs is a classic soup tureen or punch bowl. You can then take the tureen to the table when serving a salad and encourage guests to snip off the herb of their choice. Marjoram, especially the curly-leaved and golden kinds, and mint, grow well in tureens. Add chives, parsley, thyme, and basil. The plants can be dug up from the garden, used for a while, and then returned to their former site while you bring in a fresh supply.

1. Choose appropriate containers for the purpose. Look out at yard sales for large old pieces of tableware – they make ideal herb planters.

2. Remember that you don't have to choose something with drainage holes. Use the container as a cache-pot instead: keep the herbs in their pots and stand them inside it, then scatter vermiculite or shredded bark over and in between them.

MARJORAM, MINT, AND MARIGOLD

MIXED HERB BREAD

HE FASHION for unusual and interesting breads has revived the ancient idea of adding herbs to the dough. Use one herb only or make a mix. Add marigold petals too, if you like, to give added flavor and a golden coloring.

INGREDIENTS

Makes 1 x 1½ pound loaf

2 cups all-purpose flour

2 cups wholewheat flour

2 tsp salt

1 tsp dried marjoram

1 tsp dried mint

1 tsp butter or margarine

2 tsp chopped marjoram

2 tsp chopped mint

2 tsp sugar

1¼ cups warm water

2 tsp active dry yeast

❖ In a large, warmed bowl, mix the flours together with the salt and the dried herbs. Rub in the fat, then stir in the chopped fresh herbs.

❖ Dissolve the sugar in about half the warm water, and sprinkle the yeast on top. Leave for about ten minutes, until frothy.

❖ Make a hollow in the center of the flour and pour in the yeast mixture. Gradually mix with the flour, adding the remaining warm water. Finish mixing by hand until you have a soft dough.

❖ Knead the dough thoroughly on a floured board. Mold into 2 rounds, braids, or coils, and place on a baking tray. Cover with oiled plastic wrap or wax paper and leave in a warm place for about 1 hour to double in size.

❖ Bake on the middle shelf of a preheated oven at 450 degrees for 30–40 minutes.

MARIGOLD BREAD ROLLS

BREAD ROLLS are quick and easy to make, and freeze well for future use. Get some out of the freezer overnight and they will thaw out nicely to serve for breakfast. The marigold petals in this recipe give the dough an attractive color.

INGREDIENTS

Makes 12

1 tsp sugar
½ cup tepid milk
1½ tsp active dry yeast
2 cups all purpose flour
1 tsp salt
4 tbs butter or margarine
1 tbs tightly packed marigold petals
2 eggs, beaten
marigold petals, to decorate

⬦ Dissolve the sugar in the milk, sprinkle the yeast over it, and leave to froth.

⬦ Mix the flour with the salt, rub in the fat, then mix in the marigold petals.

⬦ Add the milk and half the beaten eggs. Mix until it forms a smooth dough, adding a little more milk if necessary.

⬦ Place on a floured board, cover with oiled plastic wrap or wax paper, and leave in a warm place for about 1 hour until doubled in size.

⬦ Knead the dough lightly, then cut it into 12 pieces. Shape each piece into a roll and put in rows on a greased baking sheet. Return to a warm place and allow the rolls to rise again for 20 minutes.

⬦ Brush the rolls with the beaten egg, and sprinkle marigold petals on top. Bake in a preheated oven at 425 degrees for about 15 minutes. The rolls should sound hollow when tapped.

MINT LIQUEUR

SERVE THIS unusual liqueur well chilled in small glasses as an after-dinner drink, or try it as an apéritif with tasty morsels of smoked fish. Toss it back, Russian style, in one shot.

INGREDIENTS

Makes 1 quart
1 cup tightly packed peppermint leaves
1 quart vodka
½ cup sugar

MINT JULEP

INGREDIENTS

Makes 3¼ cups
⅔ cup water
4 tbs chopped mint
2 tbs sugar
juice of 1 lemon
2 cups sparkling mineral water
½ cup bourbon

❖ Boil the water and pour it over the mint. Add the sugar and stir until dissolved. Add the lemon juice, then leave the mixture to cool.

❖ Strain into a jug, stir in the mineral water and the whiskey. Pour on to ice cubes in tall glasses, add a sprig of mint and serve.

❖ Put the mint in a wide-necked jar, and cover with the vodka.

❖ Put on the lid, shake well, then leave to steep for 2 weeks.

❖ Add the sugar and steep for 2 more weeks, shaking the jar from time to time to dissolve the sugar.

❖ Strain the liqueur into a fresh bottle, add a sprig of mint for decoration.

❖ Leave for a further 2 weeks before drinking.

MINT TEA

TIP
The best mint
to use is Moroccan
mint (*Mentha
viridis*). Failing that,
use peppermint.
Sometimes in winter
the Moroccans add
sweet marjoram to
the mint.

INGREDIENTS
Makes 3³/4 cups
*1¹/₂ tbs green tea (available from
specialist tea suppliers)
handful of whole mint leaves
³/4 cup lump sugar*

❖ Rinse out a teapot with boiling water. Put in
the tea and cover with the mint. Add the sugar
and fill the teapot with boiling water.
❖ Leave to draw for 5 minutes, taking care that the
mint does not rise above the surface of the water.
❖ Pour out into small glasses.
❖ In Morocco they make two pots of tea at a
time and pour the liquid from both pots at the
same time into the glasses.

TWO POTPOURRIS

ERFUME YOUR house with potpourris. They're easy to make, so dry as many herbs as you can and have them to hand for making potpourris. Vary the ingredients to your own taste and what you have available, but always include the orris root as it "fixes" the scent and makes your potpourri last longer.

MARJORAM, MARIGOLD, AND MINT

ARJORAM, marigold, and mint make a harmonious trio on which to base a potpourri. The spices – cloves and nutmeg – give it an exotic fragrance, while the orris root, which is derived from the white iris, preserves the perfume.

INGREDIENTS

2½ cups mixed dried marjoram leaves and marigold petals
2½ cups mixed dried lemon balm and mint
¼ cup dried lavender
2 tbs dried rosemary
2 tbs dried orris root
½ cinnamon stick
1 strip dried lemon peel
½ tsp whole cloves
½ tsp grated nutmeg
3 drops rose geranium oil
2 drops lemon oil
1 drop peppermint oil
dried marigold flowers and mint leaves, to decorate

✤ Mix all the dry ingredients, then add the oils and stir.
✤ Decorate with whole dried marigold flowers and mint leaves.

GOLDEN MARIGOLD MIX

HIS IS particularly colorful. Set it out in open bowls around the room, or stow away in fabric sachets.

INGREDIENTS

2½ cups dried yellow and orange flowers
1¼ cups dried marigold petals
2 tbs mixed dried marjoram and thyme
2 tbs senna pods
2 tbs dried orris root
2 tsp ground cinnamon
2 broken cinnamon sticks
4 tbs chopped dried lemon and orange peel
4 drops marigold oil
2 drops orange oil
1 drop lemon oil
dried marigold flowers
2 dried orange slices
2 dried lemon slices

✤ Mix all the ingredients except the citrus slices, reserving some of the dried yellow and orange flowers to top the mix.
✤ Sprinkle with the oils, mix again, then top with yellow and orange flowers, whole dried marigold flowers, and the dried orange and lemon slices.

CREAMS AND FRESHENERS

arigold's healing properties come to the fore in cosmetic creams. You will find its Latin name, *calendula* mentioned in many old herbal recipes. Even if you don't want to make your own cosmetics, it is worth while stirring a strong infusion of fresh marigold petals into a store-bought moisturizer to give it some of marigold's special qualities.

CALENDULA CREAM

HIS RICH cream is very soothing for the skin, particularly after sunburn. Use it last thing at night too, for a smooth, supple skin. The borax helps improve its keeping qualities. If you leave it out of the recipe, keep the cream in the refrigerator.

INGREDIENTS

1 tbs beeswax
1 tbs cocoa butter
1 tbs lanolin
1½ tbs marigold oil (see below right)
1 tsp glycerine
2 tbs strong infusion of marigold petals (see below)
¼ tsp borax
6 drops oil of petitgrain (optional)

✣ Infuse a handful of marigold petals in half a cup of boiling water.
✣ Melt the beeswax, cocoa butter, and lanolin together in a double boiler or in the microwave on a low setting.
✣ Warm the marigold oil with the glycerine, then stir into the beeswax mix.
✣ Keeping the mixture warm, beat in the marigold infusion and the borax, then add the oil of petitgrain and beat again.
✣ Put into small sterilized jars.

MINT FOOT FRESHENER

RY THIS old recipe for tired feet. The natural oil in the mint has a cooling effect.

INGREDIENTS

large bunch of mint
10 cups boiling water

✣ Immerse the mint in a saucepan of the boiling water. Allow to bubble for a minute or two, cover and leave to cool, then strain.
✣ Plunge your feet into this freshener while it is still tepid. Or keep the mix in a large pitcher in the fridge, and use it to sponge aching feet.

MARIGOLD OR MARJORAM OIL

You will need 1¼ cups marigold petals or marjoram leaves to 1¼ cups sunflower oil. Chop the petals or leaves finely, put into a wide-necked jar and cover with the oil which has been warmed slightly in a saucepan or in the microwave. Shake the bottle well and stand it somewhere warm, such as a sunny windowsill. Leave for at least 2 weeks, then strain the oil into a fresh bottle.

KITCHEN SACHETS

MAKE THE MOST of marjoram's insect-repellent properties by growing plenty to make into kitchen sachets or herb bags for the wardrobe and linen closet. A few dried marigold petals add color and fragrance. In the Middle Ages, it was said that a bag containing a wolf's tooth and marigold petals wrapped in bay leaves, kept under the pillow at night, would enable you to see what burglars were up to in the dark.

MATERIALS

rectangles of coarse linen or burlap 8 × 6 inches
handful of dried marjoram
small marigolds

❖ Make up small bags with the linen or burlap, gluing the side and bottom.
❖ Fill with dried herbs and glue the top.
❖ Braid strands of linen or burlap to make loops for handles and stitch in place.
❖ Add a decorative bow.

TIP

If you use a really open-weave fabric like cheesecloth, you can add fresh marigolds to your herb-filled sachets and let them dry inside. Otherwise dry your marigolds in the usual way and crumble the petals.

MARJORAM, MINT, AND MARIGOLD

Rosemary makes a handsome mature shrub even when grown in pots.

INTRODUCING ROSEMARY

ROSEMARY IS THE herb of remembrance. It is the herb of fidelity, and was placed on the graves of the dead to pledge eternal faithfulness. Rosemary is similarly linked with love and romance. The Romans used it as an aphrodisiac, and young maidens in medieval times slipped a sprig under their pillows so their true love would come to them in their dreams. Rosemary was added to the loving-cup passed round at a wedding, and the bride would give her new husband a sprig of rosemary to hold to ensure he remained faithful to her.

It has been famous throughout history and valued for many reasons – it was used to make wine, medicine and scent as well as an aromatic in the kitchen. It is said that a rosemary bush sheltered the Virgin Mary on her flight into Egypt, and that when she spread her cloak over a rosemary, the white flowers turned blue. And today in many villages in the Mediterranean region, linen is spread over rosemary bushes to dry and perfume them at the same time. It is also said that rosemary will survive for 33 years, the length of Christ's life.

The ill-fated Anne of Cleves wore rosemary in her crown on her marriage to Henry VIII.

ABOVE *Rosemary can be used to make attractive wreaths*

These properties are immortalized in Shakespeare's "Hamlet" in Ophelia's famous lines:

"There's rosemary, that's for remembrance; pray love, remember…"

Rosemary was also Napoleon's favorite perfume – he used more than a hundred bottles of rosemary water during his honeymoon alone. This aromatic, woody shrub comes from the Mediterranean where it can be found everywhere; perfuming the hillsides of Provence, growing in the ruins of temples in Greece. The word "rosemary" comes from the Latin *ros maris*, "dew of the sea," and in Italy it still grows abundantly along the coastline.

INTRODUCING RUE

RUE IS KNOWN as "the herb of grace," and it certainly makes a graceful sight in any garden with its deeply indented, blue-green leaves. It grows wild on the hillsides around the Mediterranean. Rue is a woody plant with attractive, tiny green-yellow flowers which appear in midsummer. Of the cultivated varieties, "Jackman's Blue" has dark, metallic-looking leaves, while the variegated version (*Ruta graveolens* "Variegata") is tipped with cream. Kept well-clipped, rue makes an unusual hedge around a herb garden.

Rue's strong and distinctive bitter flavor is used in after-dinner drinks such as *grappa*, the Italian brandy, and was mixed with honey to make sack, a type of mead drunk in Shakespeare's time. It was also much prized by the Greeks as one of the components of mithridate, an antidote to poisons.

The herb is said to ward off the evil effects of witchcraft and magic, and was carried in the Middle Ages as a protection from the plague. One of the ingredients of the once famous "Four Thieves Vinegar" which protected grave-robbers, it was also thought to have supernatural powers and to grant the power of second sight.

RIGHT: *A budding rue plant will develop glorious yellow flowers.*

ROSEMARY, RUE, AND ROSE

Around the house, rue makes a useful insect repellent. It is also used widely in herbal and homeopathic medicine to heal menstrual problems, rheumatism, and high blood pressure, but its toxic properties mean that if large quantities are required it must be taken under medical supervision. When you garden with rue, be sure to wash the sap off your skin as it can cause an allergic reaction that brings blisters, especially in strong sunlight.

ABOVE: *Rue goes well with brightly colored flowers in a bouquet.*

Many people believed rue improved the eyesight, and both Michelangelo and Leonardo da Vinci are said to have used infusions of it.

79

ROSEMARY, RUE, AND ROSE

INTRODUCING THE ROSE

THE ROSE HAS been called the "Queen of Flowers" and it has certainly reigned in gardens all over the world longer than any other flower. Fossilized roses more than 35 million years old have been found, and it appears in a fresco painted at Knossos in Greece dating back to 1500 BC. In ancient Persia, at the wedding feasts of the Mogul Emperors, the bride was carried in a boat along a canal filled with rosewater.

Cleopatra is said to have entertained Mark Antony on a carpet of rose petals in ancient Egypt, and Achilles used roses to decorate his shield. But it was the Romans who used roses with everything, and especially at banquets, because they believed the petals were a protection against drunkenness. At a rather boisterous party, a certain nobleman, Heliogabalus, showered his guests with so many rose petals that he accidentally suffocated seven of them. At Nero's banquets, food was sprinkled with petals and

ABOVE: *The sensual beauty of roses is a source of endless pleasure.*

guests were sprayed with rose water. His floors were lined with a thick layer of petals, and doves with rose-perfumed wings flew overhead. The rose has also been used as an emblem in battle, notably the White Rose of York and the Red Rose of Lancaster in the Wars of the Roses (1455).

Featured since the beginning of time in cookery and in medicine, the rose is used above all for perfume in which it is the most important ingredient. It takes 250 pounds of petals to produce just one ounce of essential oil.

ROSEMARY, RUE, AND ROSE

A bottle of Joy, the fragrance by Jean Patou, one of the most expensive fragrances in the world, contains the essence of almost six hundred roses.

Many families of roses are grown for their fragrance, notably centifolias which have large pink cabbage-like flowers said to contain a hundred petals. Another fragrant favorite is the damask rose, so-called because it came originally from Damascus. It was also grown at Pompeii, and produces highly-scented, soft pink ruffled blooms.

The favorite roses for a herb garden today are the gallicas, *Rosa gallica officinalis*, the apothecary's rose, with its deep red petals and *Rosa gallica* "versicolor," and "rosamundi" with its distinctive striped blooms.

BELOW: *Try massing roses together tightly in a container for maximum effect. You don't always need foliage in a flower decoration.*

The word "rose" comes from the Greek word rodon, red. Ancient roses were a deep crimson color.

PLANT CARE

ROSEMARY
Rosmarinus officinalis

Rosemary is an evergreen perennial shrub which grows up to 3 feet high and prefers a sunny, sheltered spot. It needs a well-drained soil and, once full-grown, dislikes being moved.

Rosemary is very much an all-purpose plant. You can start it from seed undercover, in a seed-tray, or in pots but it prefers some bottom heat. Take cuttings from non-flowering shoots in midsummer or late summer. If your winters are harsh, overwinter the plant in a cold frame. You can also root sprigs in spring by suspending them in a glass of water. Rosemary can also be layered. Simply peg down a low-growing branch, making a small cut in the underside of the stem, and cover with soil. Anchor it with a hoop made from a small piece of wire or a large hairpin.

RUE
Ruta graveolens

This hardy perennial grows to a height of 2 feet and likes a sunny spot. It does best in thin or poor soil.

Rue can be grown from seed, which should be mixed with a little sand when sowing as the seeds are so fine. The hybrid "Jackman's Blue," however, should be started from softwood cuttings taken in early summer.

Cut mature plants back in the spring to stop them from becoming spindly and again in mid-summer after flowering. Divide large plants when necessary. Protect variegated rue from hard frosts in winter.

1. *Set rosemary cuttings out in a tray of soil in late summer. In harsh winters, keep in a cold frame or cold greenhouse. Cuttings should have rooted by the spring.*

82

THE ROSE
Rosa

Plant roses any time from fall through early spring. Roses are "greedy feeders" so dig in plenty of manure around them. If your rose is bare-rooted, make a little mound beneath the base of the plant, then spread out the roots like the spokes of an umbrella. If your rose has been grafted onto a rootstock (look for the scar on the stem) make sure the graft is just above soil level.

Shake the plant gently from time to time as you fill in the soil around it. Tread the topsoil firmly with your feet to anchor the rose in place.

1. Plant roses on a dry day when there is no cold, prevailing wind. If the day is too cold, store the plant in a bucket of water under cover for later planting. Dig a hole wide enough to take the plant comfortably.

2. Make a little mound of soil in the hole, where the base of the plant is to go. Then put the plant in place, spreading its roots out as you go.

3. Scatter a little bone-meal around the roots then fill with soil. Check that the scar on the stem is above ground level if the rose is grafted.

4. Shake the plant from time to time as you fill in the soil, to make sure no air pockets are left around the roots. Tamp down the soil around the bush.

PRESERVING

DRYING ROSEMARY

Simply hang branches of rosemary upside down in a warm place away from direct light to dry. The faster the drying process, the more volatile oils will be left in the leaves. The flowers will be the first to dry, and can be shaken from the branch into a separate container after a day or so.

DRYING RUE

Rue tends to lose its attractive bluish hue if it is dried in the light, so keep it in as dark a place as possible. Pick individual stems and lay them on sheets of newspaper on racks. Then they can be crumbled and put into jars and used to make insect-repellent sachets or put out in bowls for the same purpose.

Branches of rue for dried flower decoration are best dried by simply standing them in a jar without water.

Rue makes a very attractive pressed plant to decorate lampshades, cards, and candles. Choose small shoots: arrange them carefully on sheets of paper and cover with absorbent kitchen paper. Use a flower-press or sandwich them between heavy books.

ABOVE: *Sprigs of rue look very attractive when pressed. Place them between sheets of absorbent paper before pressing in a flower-press.*

ABOVE: *Dried rue gives an attractive musky scent to potpourri. Dry it on racks, then crumble it.*

ABOVE: *Long-stemmed dried rosebuds make a delightful, lasting gift.*

DRYING ROSES

Rosebuds and roses should be hung upside down to dry in bunches, away from the light but in an airy place. Alternatively, they dry particularly well in silica gel, keeping both their color and their shape.

DRYING ROSE PETALS

Gather your petals when the dew has dried off in the sun. Spread them immediately on sheets of absorbent kitchen paper or newspaper, pulling the petals off separately and making sure they do not touch each other.

If you are going to use them for a potpourri, sprinkle with some of the spices you are going to use (eg, powdered clove or cinnamon) to discourage ants or any small insects that may otherwise settle on them.

Alternatively, lay out the petals on paper on trays or in a colander and put them in an oven at the lowest setting, leaving the door slightly ajar. Drying will take up to two or three days.

DRYING ROSEHIPS

Rosehips should be spread out on sheets of paper on racks to dry. Make sure they do not touch each other.

ABOVE: *A garden path lined with rosemary bushes will produce a delicious fragrance as you brush against it.*

PLANTING A HERBAL HEDGE

AROMATIC HEDGES made from herbs make a perfect fragrant edging to a narrow path. Rosemary is great for this purpose as it grows vigorously and soon thickens up to make a dense border which is easily maintained.

A rosemary hedge can be clipped to a strict shape or left to flower to provide extra color.

If you have time to spare, you can plant a rosemary hedge by taking cuttings in the fall and setting them straight into the ground. Put in twice as many as you need, in the hope that half of them will survive the winter and "take." Or you can buy container-grown plants for a speedy start.

Either way, use a length of twine to work out a straight line. Dig a row of planting holes and plant your hedge in the spring to give it a chance to get well established throughout the summer before the cold weather comes. Trim the tips once a year to encourage it to bush out.

Finish off your hedge by making rosemary standards: find a good straight plant with a single stem. Plant it in place, tie it to a bamboo stake, and encourage it to grow onward and upward by removing lower side-shoots. Once the rosemary has reached the required height, continue to remove side-shoots off the stem but allow the top to bush out, pinching out the tips of shoots to make a rounded ball shape.

1. Use twine or tightly stretched rope to mark out the site of your hedge, then fork the site over thoroughly and add some fertilizer to give your rosemary cuttings a flying start.

2. Using a purpose-cut piece of stick as a measure, set your rosemary cuttings out at intervals, putting in twice as many as you need, in case some of them fail to take.

MAKING THE MOST OF RUE

TIP

Rue grows to a medium height and likes sun, so mix it with other plants in the center rather than the back of a flowerbed, where its splendid leaves will be shown off to good effect.

LEFT: *The attractive leaves of rue mix well with other herbs.*

RUE'S GOOD-LOOKING blue-green leaves mix well with many other plants. Try it in a windowbox with tulips and other bright bulbs, or surrounding bulbs in a tub.

Rue makes a perfect foil for miniature roses, especially pink ones. It also looks good with lavender, toning in with its silver-gray leaves and emphasizing the purple-blue color of the flowers. Contrast its foliage, too, with sharp yellow tones - of golden marjoram for instance.

Clipped back well every spring, rue becomes shrubby and dense and makes a good edging for a small herb garden where larger plants would look out of scale.

Try growing rue, too, in garden urns, partnered with forget-me-nots which intensify its unusual coloring.

Variegated rue, its leaves splashed with cream, looks good planted with daffodils, tulips, and other spring flowers.

DISPLAYING ROSES

Miniature roses now come in climbing and standard, as well as conventional varieties. Grow them in pots but remember they are basically outdoor plants and should only be brought indoors to flower.

RIGHT: *Small roses grow well alongside herbs in a windowbox.*

HERE ARE so many ways of displaying the many members of the rose family. Plant old-fashioned shrub roses either side of a pathway to make a fragrant walk. Train hardy rambling roses over a frame to make a rose bower in a corner of the garden. Use climbers round the door, partnered by clematis or honeysuckle. Large-flowered roses (formerly known as hybrid tea-roses) are best confined to a bed of their own. But underplant them with something to complement their good looks and cover their bare stems – lavender or rosemary for instance. Standard roses look best in a formal garden – you could use one as the centerpiece of a herb plot. Don't forget you can buy ground-cover roses too, to scramble over a slope, and the rugosa roses make a wonderful flowering hedge. Not all roses are scented, so choose carefully. Most of the perfumed roses are red: the deeper the color the heavier the fragrance.

CHICKEN SOUP WITH ROSEMARY

DELICIOUS LEFTOVERS

Leftovers from a roast chicken can be used to make this delicious and unusual soup.

INGREDIENTS

Serves 4

2 carrots

2 onions

1 chicken carcass

2 tsp dried rosemary leaves

juice of ½ lemon

sour cream

❧ Clean and chop the carrots, and peel and chop the onions. Put in a saucepan with the chicken carcass, and add enough water to cover. Cover the pan and simmer until any meat attached to the carcass is softened and floats free.

❧ Strain off the liquid, cool it, then skim off the fat (the easiest way to do this is to first leave the liquid in the refrigerator overnight).

❧ Drop the rosemary leaves into the skimmed liquid, add the lemon juice, reheat, and serve with a swirl of sour cream.

SCRAMBLED EGGS WITH RUE

TIP
Used very sparingly, rue can give an intriguing, slightly bitter taste to egg and cheese dishes. Try adding two or three pieces of chopped leaf to an omelette or add some to a cheese sauce.

INGREDIENTS

Serves 2

4 large eggs

4 tbs butter

½ tsp minced rue

1 tbs heavy cream

2 slices lox (optional)

❖ Beat the eggs and season them with salt and pepper. Using a small, nonstick saucepan, heat half the butter until it begins to foam, swirling it around the bottom of the pan. Pour in the eggs and stir vigorously with a fork, scooping the egg away from the sides.

❖ Take the pan off the heat while the egg is still liquid, stir in the chopped rue, the rest of the butter, and the cream. Serve immediately with slivers of lox, if liked.

ROSE PETAL LIQUEUR

HERB AND flower liqueurs are delightful to serve either before or after a meal. If you prefer you can substitute vodka or rum for the brandy.

INGREDIENTS

Makes 1 bottle

3 cups rose petals
strip of lemon rind
1 bottle brandy
1½ cups sugar

❖ Choose roses that have not been sprayed with insecticides or polluted by exhaust fumes. Rinse and carefully dry the petals if they are dusty.
❖ Put the rose petals and the lemon rind in a wide-mouthed screwtop jar.
❖ Cover with the brandy, seal, and leave in a cool place for 28 days, shaking occasionally.
❖ Add the sugar, and leave for 14 days, shaking well once or twice a day, so that the sugar is dissolved.
❖ Strain off the petals and discard them. Decant the brandy into a sterilized bottle. Seal tightly and leave to mature for at least a month in a cool, dark place before using.

ROSEHIP GIN

HIS IS A variation on the old-fashioned sloe gin of our grandmother's time. If you make it in the fall when the rosehips are in the hedgerows, your rosehip gin will be ready in time for Christmas.

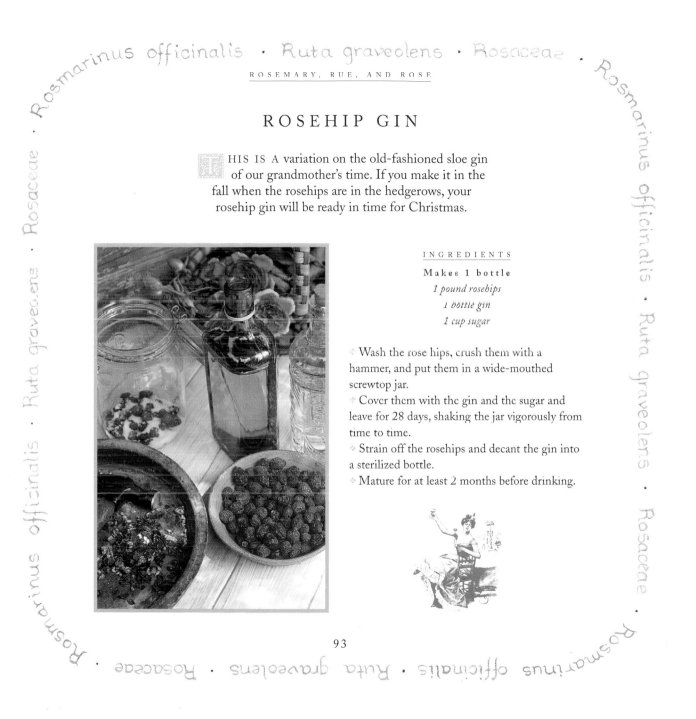

INGREDIENTS
Makes 1 bottle
1 pound rosehips
1 bottle gin
1 cup sugar

❧ Wash the rose hips, crush them with a hammer, and put them in a wide-mouthed screwtop jar.

❧ Cover them with the gin and the sugar and leave for 28 days, shaking the jar vigorously from time to time.

❧ Strain off the rosehips and decant the gin into a sterilized bottle.

❧ Mature for at least 2 months before drinking.

ROSEMARY, RUE, AND ROSE

SCENTED PILLOWS

BOTH ROSEMARY and roses retain their scent for a long
time when dried, and make delightful scented pillows.
Make them on a small scale to tuck behind your head when
traveling, to make your journey more comfortable. They can
also be slipped under your pillow at night.

MATERIALS

*2 squares fabric the same size
approximately 8 the dried potpourri
trimming for the edge
2 cheesecloth squares 1 inch smaller than
the fabric above (optional)*

*1. Right sides together,
sew the two squares of
fabric together, leaving
a gap for filling.
Turn right side out, press.
If you are using the
cheesecloth as an inner
sachet, sew the sides
together as above.
Fill the sachet with herbs
and stitch up the gap in
the seam, insert into the
cushion and handstitch
the gap in the seam.
If you are not using a
sachet, fill the cushion
with potpourri and
slipstitch the gap.
Sew the trimming in
place round the edges
to hide the seams.*

HUNGARY WATER

ERBS HAVE BEEN used throughout the ages to make fragrant toilet waters to freshen and scent the body. Flowering tops of rosemary and roses macerated in alcohol are the basic ingredients of Hungary Water, one of the most ancient perfumes. It was invented in 1370 by a hermit for the 72-year-old Dionna Izabella, the Queen of Hungary, to make "a young face exceedingly beautiful, an old face very tolerable." She claimed that it so improved her health and strength that "on beholding my beauty the King of Poland desired to marry me…"

INGREDIENTS

Makes 3¾ cups

4 tbs rosemary, preferably flowering tops

4 tbs scented rose petals

4 tbs mint

2 tbs grated lemon rind

1¼ cups rosewater

1¼ cups orangeflower water

1¼ cups vodka

1. Pound the rosemary leaves with the rose petals and mint. Add the grated lemon rind. Transfer to a wide-mouthed jar, and cover with the rosewater, orangeflower water, and vodka.

2. Leave to steep for 2 weeks, then strain into a bottle and seal tightly. Leave to mature for 1 month before using.

EAU DE COLOGNE

AU DE COLOGNE was invented in the 18th century. If you have difficulty in finding bergamot leaves you could use 10 drops of the essential oil instead.

INGREDIENTS

Makes 1¹/₂ cups

4 tbs bergamot leaves
8 tbs rosemary leaves
grated rind of 1 orange
grated rind of 1 lemon
3 drops neroli oil
1¹/₂ cups vodka

❧ Put all the ingredients in a wide-mouthed jar and cover with the vodka. Leave to macerate for 3 weeks, shaking the jar from time to time.

❧ Strain off into a clean bottle and leave for at least 2 weeks to mature.

COSMETIC CREAMS

BOTH ROSEMARY and rose are essential ingredients for many beauty creams. Rosemary is good for the hair, too. Pour boiling water over a handful of rosemary leaves, allow it to cool, strain, and use it as a final rinse. It is best for brunettes as, like sage, it tends to darken the hair. For an extra strong effect, mix rosemary with purple sage. Test it on a lock of hair to check the color before using.

DR GALEN'S COLD CREAM

THIS SIMPLE recipe for cold cream is more than 1800 years old, and was invented by the great physician, Galen, in Greece.

INGREDIENTS

4 tbs olive oil
4 tbs perfumed rose petals
1 tbs beeswax
still spring water

1. Place the oil in a double boiler or in a bowl in the microwave. Heat until it is warm, then pack with rose petals. Cover and leave as long as you can – a minimum of 4 days. Strain.

2. Heat the beeswax, then blend in the perfumed oil and stir until the mixture cools. Beat in enough spring water to give the consistency you need.

Rosmarinus officinalis · Ruta graveolens · Rosaceae · Rosmarinus officinalis · Ruta graveolens · Rosaceae · Rosmarinus officinalis · Ruta graveolens · Rosaceae · Rosmarinus officinalis · Ruta graveolens · Rosaceae

ROSEMARY, RUE, AND ROSE

ROSE MOISTURE CREAM

INGREDIENTS
1 tsp beeswax
1 tsp lanolin
1 tbs almond oil
1/4 tsp wheatgerm oil
1/4 tsp borax
3 tbs rosewater
6 drops rose oil

◈ Melt the beeswax and the lanolin together with the almond and wheatgerm oils in a double-boiler or in a bowl in the microwave on a low setting.
◈ Dissolve the borax in the rosewater and beat into the mixture.
◈ Stir in the rose oil as it thickens.

RICH ROSE POTPOURRI

N THIS layered potpourri, the scents of the different layers of dried herbs combine with time to give a delicious fragrance. Keep the potpourri for at least six weeks before use. Keeping it well sealed will improve the scent.

INGREDIENTS
2½ cups dried pink and red rose petals
2½ cups dried mint leaves
4 tbs dried rue sprigs
2½ cups dried red rosebuds
4 tbs dried rosemary flowers and leaves
¼ vanilla bean
2 tbs orris root
2 tsp ground cinnamon
½ tsp ground cloves
5 drops rose oil
5 drops rosemary oil
1 drop patchouli oil

They are not long, the
days of wine and roses
Out of a misty dream
Our path emerges for a while, then closes
Within a dream.
ERNEST DOWSON

1. Put the dried herbs into separate bowls. Chop the vanilla pod finely, mix together with the orris root, cinnamon, and cloves. Mix the oils together in a cup.

2. Put the dried herbs in a wide-mouthed jar in layers, starting with rose petals, then a layer of mint and rue, then rosebuds, and finally the rosemary. On each layer, sprinkle over a little of the orris, cinnamon, and clove mixture, and a drop or two of the oil mixture. Finish with a layer of rose petals.

Salvia
officinalis
Tricolor

Salvia
officinalis
Purpurea

Salvia
lavandulifolia

Salvia
rutilans

Sal
offi
icteri

Salvia
sclarea

Sage comes in many attractive guises.

Salvia
officinalis

INTRODUCING SAGE

HE WORD SAGE comes from the Latin *salvere*, to be saved or preserved, while the English name refers to wisdom. The Romans considered sage to be sacred and it has always been rated as one of the great healing herbs of all time. There is an old belief that where sage flourishes in a garden the woman rules, and another that the plant grows or withers according to the prosperity of the master of the house.

Known to promote a long and healthy life, the 18th-century writer John Evelyn said it was a plant "endu'd with so many wonderful properties as that the assiduous use of it is said to render men immortal." The ancient Chinese thought so highly of it that they would trade three chests of China tea (the dried leaves of a form of *Camellia*) for one of sage leaves.

"How can man grow old who has sage in his garden?" says an ancient proverb. There is also a saying that "he that would live for aye, must eat Sage in May." Italian peasants to this day eat it in that month to preserve their health. It is also said to improve brain power.

Found growing in wild profusion in its native habitat, the Mediterranean, sage can stand on its own as a decorative plant in any flowerbed and will survive the winter.

CHINA TEA

Tea is made from an evergreen shrub called Camellia thea. *The leaves are picked, air-dried, then roasted, rolled, then dried again. The flowery taste of some China teas comes from the addition of dried jasmine flowers.*

103

INTRODUCING SORREL

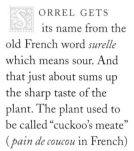

ORREL GETS its name from the old French word *surelle* which means sour. And that just about sums up the sharp taste of the plant. The plant used to be called "cuckoo's meate" (*pain de coucou* in French) because it was believed by country people that cuckoos feasted on it to clear their throats.

In the time of Henry VIII, sorrel was a favorite vegetable at the king's court. Some people believe, incidentally, that it was the tiny leaves of wood sorrel rather than the shamrock, which St Patrick, the patron saint of Ireland, used to demonstrate the trinity. John Evelyn wrote in 1720 that sorrel "cools the liver … and in the making of sallets imparts a greatful quickness to the rest as supplying the want of oranges and lemons."

Sorrel's distinctive lemony flavor has come back into favor in recent years for fashionable sauces in the *Nouvelle Cuisine* mode. Tasting something like spinach but with a much stronger citrus kick, it needs to be used in small quantities as a flavoring rather than as a vegetable. It is very difficult to find in the stores and markets but can be grown with great ease in your garden. Buckler leaf or French sorrel, *Rumex scutatus*, has wider leaves like arrowheads, and is preferred by some for its milder flavor.

Sorrel comes from the dock family, which includes rhubarb. Use its sharp flavor as a refreshing counterfoil to rich creamy food, as the Romans did. It makes an attractive sauce to go with greasy foods like duck or goose. Laplanders use it instead of rennet to curdle milk for making cheese.

Try it as a cooling drink: Culpeper claimed that it refreshed "overspent spirits."

COOLING DRINK

Sorrel is seldom served as a drink these days because its rather sharp, acrid taste is harsh on the tongue – but try this refreshing beverage. Make up a solution of one tablespoonful of minced leaves in six tablespoons of boiling water. Allow it to steep, strain, then mix with a bottle of white wine.

Left to run to seed, sorrel's dark-green leaves make a handsome backdrop to lovage and chives.

INTRODUCING SAVORY

SHRUBBY SAVORY, with its distinctive peppery taste, is a native of the Mediterranean where it grows wild on the hillsides. The Romans grew it near their beehives in the hope of getting some much prized savory honey, which they used as an aphrodisiac. They used savory vinegar in the way we use mint sauce today with lamb, and their armies were responsible for taking it to northern Europe.

There are two kinds of savory, the summer variety (*Satureia hortensis*) and the perennial winter variety (*Satureia montana*), and both of them come from the southern countries of Europe. Both types of savory were on the list of plants taken across the Atlantic to the United States by the Pilgrim Fathers. Winter savory is frequently grown in gardens today as a useful edging plant for a summer border. It can also be found as a creeping version (*Satureia montana reprandra*), which looks good on rockeries.

Culpeper wrote that it "Quickens dull spirits in lethargy," while Parkinson suggested mixing dry savory with bread crumbs to give a "quicker relish to fish and meat".

The finer of the two varieties, and the one most commonly used for culinary purposes, is summer savory which has a distinctive peppery, rather bitter flavor, not unlike that of thyme. It is used traditionally with beans of any kind, and gives an extra zing to fresh pea soup. In Italy it is used in sausage-making, especially the famous salami. Above all, it is often used to partner goat's cheese, with which it seems to have a particular affinity.

Widely used at one time in medicine as treatment for everything from poor eyesight to tinnitus, it continues to be grabbed by gardeners as an emergency treatment for wasp- or bee-stings.

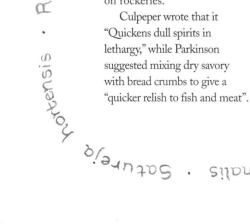

Pot-grown savories make handsome indoor plants.

SAGE, SORREL, AND SAVORY

PLANT CARE
SAGE
Salvia officinalis

S AGE IS A perennial plant and an evergreen, and will grow to a height of around 2 feet. It likes a fertile soil if it can get it, and some sun, but otherwise will survive in almost any garden surroundings, as long as the ground is well drained. And, provided you cut it back to base in the spring, it will turn in time into a small, good-looking bush that will flourish for many years.

Sow common and clary sage in the spring where they are to grow. Take cuttings from the variegated varieties as they do not always grow true to form from seed. Plant out the cuttings in the fall. Old sage plants which have become "leggy" can be layered very successfully by pegging a branch down and covering it with soil. Plants need to be replaced every 4–7 years.

1. Take cuttings from mid-summer to the end of summer. Using a clean sharp knife, cut off a non-flowering sideshoot 4–6 inches long. Cut off the stem just below a set of leaves.

2. Dip the end of the cutting in water then in rooting powder, shake off the excess, and plant the cutting firmly in a pot of suitable compost.

108

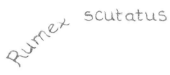
SORREL
Rumex acetosa, Rumex scutatus

ORREL, *R. acetosa*, is a lush green perennial which usually grows up to 18 inches high, but can reach 2 feet in a wet summer. Sorrel will grow almost anywhere, but prefers a moist acid soil and some shade.

Sow the seed in spring and thin the seedlings out to 9 inches apart as they grow. A little sorrel goes a long way – a dozen plants will be more than enough. As the flowers appear, cut the stems to the ground and fresh shoots will emerge. Divide the plants regularly in spring or fall, as if they become too tightly packed, they will attract the attention of snails. French or buckler leaf sorrel, *R. scutatus*, grows to a height of 12–18 inches. Unlike *R. acetosa*, it prefers a dry soil. Sow the seed in shallow drills, then thin the seedlings first to 3 inches then to 6 inches apart as they grow. Pinch out the tiny green flowers to encourage new growth.

1. To thin the seedlings, lift and replant 9 inches apart, taking care not to damage the delicate roots. Alternatively, simply uproot unwanted seedlings for use in salads.

SAVORY
Satureia montana, Satureia hortensis

INTER SAVORY, *S. montana*, is a shrubby perennial that keeps its leaves on most of the year round. It grows to a height of about 12 inches tall and likes to be in full sun in a well-drained soil.

Sow the seed where it is to grow in early fall or in the spring. Thin the seedlings to 6–9 inches apart when they are large enough to handle. Alternatively, divide the roots in early spring, or take cuttings in early summer. winter savory needs to be replaced every 2–3 years as it becomes very woody.

Summer savory, *S. hortensis*, is a half-hardy annual which grows from 8–12 inches high. Like winter savory, it prefers the sun and it must have a well-drained soil. Sow summer savory in the spring where it is to grow. For a winter supply, sow in the early fall to grow in pots in the greenhouse. Although summer savory is an annual, once you have raised a patch from seed it will self-sow from then onward, giving you a fresh crop of plants each spring.

TIP
Take cuttings of winter savory in the fall, pot them up, and bring them indoors for fresh young growth in winter.

Bunches of drying herbs look attractive in the kitchen.

PRESERVING

ERBS CAN BE preserved in many ways. The more pungent varieties are good steeped in oil, while others, including sorrel, can be packed between layers of salt. Don't forget to use them, too, in pickles and chutneys. They should always be added toward the end of the cooking process.

PRESERVING SAGE

As sage is a perennial plant you can pick it all year round without having to resort to drying it, but some people prefer the stronger flavor that dried leaves give.

Strip away any leaves on the stems you have cut that may be turning yellow, and tie the sage in bundles of five or six stems at a time. Hang the bundles, tips down, in a dry, warm place such as near a furnace or radiator or on a shady porch in summer. After about a week the leaves should be dry and crisp. They can then be crumbled by hand, or sieved then stored in screw-top jars.

You may want to dry decorative variegated sage, purple sage, or tricolor sage for part of a winter flower arrangement. The easiest way to do this is to choose some long stems and simply put them in a jar with no water. Kept in a warm, well-ventilated place away from the light, they will dry out very successfully and will make an attractive display.

PRESERVING SORREL

Sorrel cannot be dried but can be frozen very successfully. Simply blanch the leaves briefly in boiling water, drain them, pat them partly dry between two pieces of kitchen paper towel, then pack them in plastic bags. As the flavor of sorrel is so pungent, it pays to mark the weight of the fresh-picked leaves on the packet to make sure you do not add too much to a dish and overwhelm it.

PRESERVING SAVORY

Savory does not dry particularly well, and is best frozen. The easiest way to do this is to strip the tiny leaves off the stems, fill ice cube trays with them, top up with water, and freeze. You then have cubes of flavor to use in broths, soups, and stews. Alternatively take whole sprigs, pack them in plastic sandwich bags and store them in the freezer.

111

SAGE, SORREL, AND SAVORY

112

SAGE, SORREL, AND SAVORY

A HERBAL TOWER

NE OF THE most attractive ways of getting a number of herbs into a relatively small space is to grow a herbal tower. A strawberry-barrel can just as easily be a herb-barrel, or you could use clay strawberry-pots on a smaller scale. Or you could make your own tower using a large plastic garbage bag. If the plastic is relatively thin, use two, one inside the other.

HIGH-RISE HERBS

There are many kinds of flower towers on the market now that do equally well for herbs. Some slot into one another to make mini-skyscrapers; others can be fixed to a wall, or allowed to hang from a bracket. Try making your own. Use your ingenuity – a discarded linen basket could have holes cut in its sides to take plants; a piece of plastic drainpipe could easily have holes bored in it, too, for the same purpose.

LEFT: *Try growing herbs in a strawberry pot.*

1. Decide where the tower is to go, site the bag, and fill with good quality compost, rolling down the top of the bag to the required height. Make drainage holes in the bottom and sit it on pieces of tile so there is a gap between the bag and the ground. If you are using a large bag, put a piece of drainpipe down the center temporarily, and fill it with pebbles or stones. As you fill the compost around it, pull the pipe up, and eventually out. This gives the bag a very effective drainage system.

2. Using sharp scissors, make holes in the side where you want the herbs to go, creating a diamond pattern. Then push in the herbs, roots first. In time they should cover the plastic.

TIP

When planting any kind of herb-barrel or tower, it is vital that you make sure that it is placed on level ground. Otherwise you will find when you water it that one side will get plenty of moisture while the other may go without.

HERB BUTTERS

HERB BUTTERS are very easy to make and will store for a long time in the refrigerator, indefinitely in the freezer. Make a selection to keep on hand. Chill the butter, cut and wrap in small segments, or save in small pots so that you can defrost it quickly and easily to liven up a meal. A pot of chilled herb butter is delicious on broiled steak or chicken, and on fish too. The flavor is released as the butter melts and mingles with the cooking juices.

SAVORY BUTTER

Spread this butter on bread to go with cheeses of all kinds. Savory goes well with garlic, so add some to the mix if the idea appeals to you.

INGREDIENTS
Makes ¹/₂ cup
¹/₂ cup butter
2 tbs minced savory

❖ Melt the butter slowly in a saucepan, add the chopped savory, and cook for two minutes, stirring constantly. Take the pan off the heat, and leave to stand for 30 minutes.
❖ Reheat and strain off the herb. Pour the butter into little ceramic pots and decorate with fresh sprigs of savory.

SAGE BUTTER

It is best to used dried rather than fresh sage for this butter, otherwise the texture of fresh leaves makes it difficult to spread.

INGREDIENTS
Makes ¹/₂ cup
¹/₂ cup butter
1 tsp lemon juice
2 tsp dried sage

❖ Soften the butter with a fork and work in the lemon juice drop by drop, then the dried sage. Put the mix in the refrigerator to chill until firm.
❖ Turn out onto parchment or wax paper, and shape into a square before serving. Or cut into strips, wrap each one separately, and freeze.

115

BARBECUE HERBS

N MANY of the countries of the Middle East, sage is used in the classic kabob, with lamb, tomatoes, and onions. Thread young sage leaves onto skewers, alternating them with the other ingredients to give a delicious aroma while they cook, and a wonderful flavor when you eat them.

LAMB AND ZUCCHINI KABOBS

INGREDIENTS

Serves 6

1½ pounds boned shoulder of lamb
1 shallot, finely chopped
1 clove garlic, crushed
2 tbs minced parsley
6 tbs olive oil
4 tbs sage vinegar or
dry white wine
2 tbs lemon juice
6 small zucchini
4 tbs butter
2 bayleaves
12 small salad tomatoes
6 small onions
3 tbs brandy
handful of
sage leaves

⬧ Cut the lamb into 1-inch cubes. Mix the shallot with the garlic, parsley, olive oil, vinegar, lemon juice, and bayleaves. Add the meat and leave to marinate for half a day, then take out and leave to drain.

⬧ Cut the zucchini into thick slices. Sauté them in the butter in a heavy-based skillet until they are just beginning to soften. Remove and drain.

⬧ Grease 6 large skewers. Thread on the lamb, zucchini, and tomatoes, interlacing them with the sage leaves. Season with salt and pepper, and brush with the butter remaining in the pan.

⬧ Cook the kabobs 4 inches from the coals, turning from time to time, for up to 15 minutes or until the lamb is just cooked through.

⬧ Arrange the kabobs on a flameproof dish, add the brandy, and ignite it.

⬧ Serve with pita bread or plain white rice, accompanied by a tomato-and-onion salad.

BARBECUED PORK WITH SAVORY, SORREL, AND SAGE SAUCE

INGREDIENTS

Serves 8

6 tbs meat broth

1 tbs French mustard

6 tbs plain yogurt

juice of ½ lemon

1 tbs minced sage

2 tbs minced sorrel

1 tbs minced savory

⅔ cup mayonnaise

8 pork chops

salad of mixed green leaves, to serve

❖ Put the meat broth into a blender with the mustard, yogurt, lemon juice, sage, sorrel, and savory. Blend to a purée. Beat in the mayonnaise, and put into the refrigerator to chill.

❖ Broil the chops over hot coals for 10–12 minutes each side, until thoroughly cooked through.

❖ Serve them with the salad over which the sauce has been spooned.

TIP

If you are afraid that your barbecued meat may not cook right through, give it a few moments in a microwave oven immediately beforehand.

Rumex scutatus · Salvia officinalis · Satureja hortensis
SAGE, SORREL, AND SAVORY

AN INDOOR TREE

HIS ATTRACTIVE topiary tree is made from oasis, a type of florist's foam which is easy to use. Dried sage twigs look very decorative in mixed dried flower arrangements; save some of the more decorative varieties to act as a foil for flowers and grasses.

MATERIALS
*1 oasis ball about 5 inches
in diameter
1 cone-shaped piece of
oasis 7–8 inches tall
glue
thick bamboo or stout,
straight twig at least
18 inches long
clay pot
polythene
plaster of Paris
spaghnum moss
dried sage twigs*

1. Slice a section from the ball and the base of the cone to create 2 flat surfaces of equal diameter, then glue them together.

2. Push the bamboo into the bottom of the ball. Line the pot with polythene. Make up a plaster of Paris mix and pour into the pot. Push the bamboo into the plaster and leave until set, making sure it is vertical.

3. Cover the oasis with spaghnum moss, gluing it in place, then glue the sage twigs in place to completely cover the tree. Trim the polythene and cover with moss.

TIP
Save sage for potpourri, too. The leaves help to bulk out a mixture, and their aroma mixes in well with more exotic scents.

SAGE, SORREL, AND SAVORY

119

SAGE FOR HEALTHY HAIR

AN INFUSION of sage makes a rinse for brunettes that will help disguise gray hairs. Add some rosemary leaves to turn it into a hair tonic.

SAGE HAIR COLORANT

THIS MIX of sage and China tea helps to restore the color of hair that is "pepper-and-salt", ie going gray. The color should last for six shampoos. It is advisable to do a test patch first, to make sure you like the color.

INGREDIENTS
China tea
1 tsp dried sage or 1 tbs fresh sage

❖ Make up a strong brew of China tea.
❖ Add a tablespoonful of fresh sage or a teaspoonful of dried sage to the tea while it is still very hot.

❖ Allow to cool, strain, then, using rubber gloves so your hands are not stained, rub it into damp, shampooed hair with your fingertips.

SAGE AND ROSEMARY HAIR RINSE

AN INFUSION of sage makes a rinse for brunettes that will help disguise gray hairs. Add some rosemary leaves to turn it into a hair tonic.

Make up a strong infusion of whole sage stems with their leaves. Pour boiling water over them and bruise them with a wooden spoon.

Strain and bottle when the mixture has cooled and refrigerate it. Rub a little into the roots of your hair each day.

SAGE, SORREL, AND SAVORY

HERBAL DYES

ERBS HAVE been used for dyes and colorings ever since the days when the Ancient Britons painted themselves with woad. Sorrel has been used since medieval times to dye cloth. If you use the roots of sorrel you should get a dusky pink coloring, while the leaves and stems produce a subtle yellow. Use only natural fibers such as silk, wool, cotton, or linen for dyeing; man-made fibers simply will not "take."

❀ First wash your material thoroughly. If you are using virgin wool you will need to wash it several times to remove the natural lanolin. End with a final rinse in vinegar.

❀ You will need to add something to "fix" the color. Alum is the mordant that is normally used with sorrel. Buy it from a pharmacy; you will need 2 tbs for every 1 pound material.

❀ Use an equal weight of sorrel to the weight of the fabric, ie 1 pound herb to every 1 pound cloth.

❀ Dissolve the alum in a little hot water, put it in a dye bath or bucket then add another 20 quarts water. Put in the fabric to be dyed, bring very slowly to the boil and simmer for one hour - the water temperature should be about 125 degrees. Rinse the fabric and it is ready for dyeing.

❀ Chop the leaves of the sorrel or crush the roots with a hammer. Put it in a bag made from cheesecloth or a piece of old nylon net curtain. Leave to soak overnight in a large preserving pan, enamel bowl, or bucket.

❀ Then bring the mix to the boil and simmer for up to 3 hours, or until the water has taken on the color you want.

❀ Take out the bag of sorrel, cool the mix then immerse the fabric and simmer for one hour.

❀ Leave the fabric to cool in the water, then take out, and rinse in warm then cold water. Finally, hang out to dry.

TIP
**If you are dyeing wool to
make a sweater, always do an extra
hank so you have yarn left for repairs.
You will never be able to duplicate
the exact shade again.**

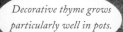

Decorative thyme grows particularly well in pots.

INTRODUCING THYME

HIS IS ONE of the great culinary herbs which grows wild all over Europe – you will smell its perfume underfoot while walking on the hills in the South of France, Italy, or Greece, where it has been used in cooking since ancient times. It is a plant that is much loved by bees. Owners of beehives were said to be able to tell with perfect accuracy what their annual honey yields would be "by the plentifull or small number of flowers growing and appearing in Thyme about the summer solstice."

The name derives from the Greek *thumos,* meaning courage, and it was believed in ancient times that to take a draught of thyme would give you courage in battle. The Greeks also used it as an incense in their temples. Among the Greeks, to refer to someone as "smelling of thyme" was an expression of praise. It is also believed that the famous honey of Mount Hymettus, near Athens, came from bees fed on wild thyme, which still grows in the region today.

The ancient Egyptians used oil of thyme for embalming bodies, and it was believed that if anyone came into a house in which someone was ill, bearing a sprig of thyme, the patient would die within three days.

Because of its antiseptic properties, thyme was also used as a

powerful fumigant. The Roman writer Pliny said that when thyme was burned "it puts to flight all venomous creatures." The Romans also used it to flavor cheese and to make cordials, and they were among the first people to use thyme in the kitchen, though the Greeks were known to have marinated sprigs of thyme in white wine as an aphrodisiac.

In medieval Britain, thyme was believed to have magical properties, and it was thought that if you drank a potion made from it you would be able to see the fairies. It was also a symbol of good luck, and ladies embroidered a sprig of thyme with a bee hovering over it as a symbol of courage on the scarves they presented to their knights.

123

INTRODUCING TANSY

HE NAME TANSY is thought to come from the Greek *athanaton* meaning immortal, probably because it stays in flower for such a long time. But it may also be so named because the ancient Greeks used it to preserve the bodies of their dead. It thrives naturally both in Europe and Asia and may be hard to find in stores, though specialist herb farms carry it. Once established, tansy's vigorous roots extend over great distances.

Tansy's fly-repellent properties made it a popular strewing herb in the time of Thomas Tusser, the 16th-century expert in good husbandry, when its leaves were laid on the floor together with rue. It was used in insect-repellent potpourris, too.

Tansy has always been associated with Easter, and tansy cakes or "tansies" were eaten in medieval times. These custards, which became symbolic, were made from young leaves of the plant cooked with eggs, and were thought to purify the body after the restricted diet that people ate during Lent. A herbalist of the day claimed that tansy counteracted the ill-effects which the "moist and cold constitution of the winter has made on people." Later, tansy took on another significance, being eaten on Easter Day as a remembrance of the bitter herbs eaten by the Jews at Passover.

At one time a glass of tansy was thought to counteract hysteria, while in Scotland it was considered a cure for gout. Today, it is sometimes used as a compress to relieve rheumatic joints and also to stop sprains from swelling.

The herb has fern-like leaves and yellow button flowers, from which it gets the common English name of bachelors' buttons, and makes a handsome addition to a flower bed. It is a strong grower, however, and needs plenty of space.

In Finland, tansy is used as a dye, yielding a bright green coloring. Tansy flowers keep their color very well when they are dried, provided that you hang them away from bright sunlight.

It is thought that tansy was first taken to America by the Pilgrim Fathers; certainly it nows grows wild throughout the U.S.

LEFT: *Tansy has attractive yellow button flowers.*
BELOW: *Dried tansy is attractive in winter flower decorations.*

TANSY AMBER CAKES

Blanch a pound of Almonds, steep them in a pint of cream, pound them in a mortar, add to them the yolks of twelve and whites of six eggs, put in half a pint of juice of spinage and a quarter of a pint of juice of Tansy, add to it grated Bread; sweeten it with sugar to your palate fry it in sweet Butter and keep stirring in the Pan till it is of a good thickness strew sugar over it and serve it up.–

From *The Receipt Book of John Nott*,
COOK TO THE DUKE OF BOLTON, 1723

INTRODUCING TARRAGON

HE WORD TARRAGON comes from the ancient Latin word for dragon – *dracunculus*. It has been known throughout history as the dragon herb, supposedly named for the tortuous shape of its roots. It was the royal herb of the Persian kings who drank it mixed with fennel as an aphrodisiac. It was Marie Antoinette's favorite herb, too. She assigned a royal gardener to the sole task of cultivating it and sent a lady-in-waiting every day wearing white kid gloves to pick perfect leaves for her salad.

Tarragon's native habitat is southern Europe. It first made its appearance in English gardens at the time of Henry VIII. In some old English herbals, it is listed as Serpentyne and was thought to cure a wide range of ailments from "breaking of veines" to head, heart, or liver problems, probably because, like most herbs, it contains many vitamins. More recently, it has been used as a herbal cure for toothache and to help combat insomnia.

A member of the pretty *artemisia* family, tarragon comes in two forms – French and Russian. While the Russian tarragon (*Artemisia dracunculus "indora"*) grows more strongly and is hardier, the taste is inclined to be coarse. The French variety is best for fine flavor, though it is more difficult to grow since it may die in a hard winter.

A little tarragon goes a long way in cooking for it has a faint flavor of aniseed. It is best known for the famous French dish *Poulet à l'Estragon* (Chicken in Tarragon), and in two classic sauces, *Sauce Tartare* and *Sauce Béarnaise*.

THYME, TANSY, AND TARRAGON

LEFT: *Tarragon is particularly suited to egg dishes, and with onions and garlic.*

TIP
Tarragon goes well with eggs, if it is used sparingly, and makes a classic flavoring for vinegar.

ABOVE: *Keep some tarragon in a pot indoors to prolong its growing season.*

127

PLANT CARE

THYME
Thymus
⤴

This small bushy perennial is a native of hot dry hillsides, so it needs well-drained soil and as much sun as possible. Thyme prefers some protection from the wind. Upright thymes reach up to around 12 inches in height; creeping thymes just an inch or two.

Sow the seed in late spring where it is to grow then thin out the seedlings of most thymes to about 1 foot apart. Creeping thymes should be placed 8 inches apart.

If a patch of thyme looks dead in the center and you don't want to divide it, try heaping a spadeful of soil over it, and it should regenerate. Despite the fact that thyme can handle drought, young plants should be watered frequently until they have settled.

TIP
All thymes should be cut back after flowering. Trim them with garden shears. If your thyme forms over-large clumps after a year or so, these should be split up, trimmed of dead wood and re-planted.

TANSY
Tanacetum vulgare
⤴

A hardy perennial, tansy grows to 3 feet high. It will thrive almost anywhere, but does not like a waterlogged soil.

Sow tansy in the spring. The seed is almost like dust, so it is better started indoors. Sow the seed on the surface of a seed-tray then cover with a light dusting of potting mixture.

Grown tansy plants can be divided in the fall or spring. Cut them back after they have flowered. Tansy makes a handsome foliage plant in a mixed border, particularly among tall, strong-growing perennials such as goldenrod (*Solidago*).

However, if it is left unchecked it can tend to take over and swamp other more delicate plants in the bed, so divide it frequently.

The easiest way to propagate thyme is by layering. Peg an outside branch to the ground, using a large bobbypin or piece of bent wire, then heap soil over the center of it.

Large clumps of tansy benefit from being divided into smaller plants. Split the root, using a sharp spade.

ABOVE: *Harvest thyme frequently
to keep it green and bushy.*

TARRAGON
Artemisia dranunculus/dranunculoides

Of the two kinds of tarragon, the best, French tarragon (*A. dranunculus*), is a tender perennial plant which grows to about 3 feet in height and is best grown in a pot that can be put somewhere frost-free in winter. The taller, coarser Russian tarragon (*A. dranunculoides*) on the other hand is hardy in cooler climates and reaches a height of 4 feet or more.

Both like a sheltered, sunny place to grow with a rich, well-drained soil.

Sow Russian tarragon from seed, starting it off in seed-trays then transferring the seedlings to the garden when they are large enough. French tarragon can only be started from cuttings. Root cuttings are best.

TIP
Tarragon hates being overshadowed by the leaves of other, larger plants, so make sure it gets plenty of sun to itself.

*Pull off a piece of root
with nodules on it and
raise in potting mixture.*

PRESERVING

PRESERVING THYME

Thyme does not freeze very well but can be dried very successfully. Make it up into small bunches and suspend them somewhere away from the sun, so that their essential oils do not evaporate in the heat. Choose a well-ventilated place, as thyme takes a long time to dry and the leaves could rot in damp surroundings.

Once the leaves feel crisp, rub them off the stems (which can be saved to put on an open fire in winter) straight into dry jars. Save some leaves to crush under a rolling pin and use as a seasoning powder – try a pinch in egg dishes, for instance.

PRESERVING TANSY

The best way to dry tansy for sachets is to spread it out on racks in a dry, well-ventilated place where it will quickly become crisp. For perfumed powders, crumple the leaves into tiny pieces. For potpourri, break the leaves into pieces. Tansy flowers take longer to dry than the leaves but keep their color well to use in wreaths and potpourri. Cut them into sprigs and dry them on newspaper on a rack. Once dried, store both leaves and flowers in paper bags ready for use.

PRESERVING TARRAGON

Tarragon leaves can be quickly dried in the oven on the lowest possible setting. However, they tend to lose flavor this way so it is better to preserve tarragon by freezing sprigs instead: slip them into clear plastic sandwich bags, exclude the air by flattening them with the palm of your hand, then put in the freezer. There is no doubt that the best way to capture tarragon's aniseed-like flavor is to use it in oils and vinegars.

THYME, TANSY, AND TARRAGON

ABOVE: *Thyme in bunches ready for drying.*
LEFT: *Preparing tarragon for freezing.*

131

A WAGONWHEEL

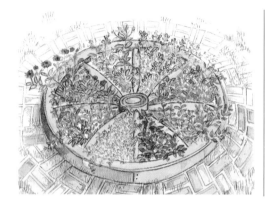

AN OLD wagonwheel makes a perfect way to show off herbs. You could paint it a bright color – turquoise for instance, and then put your plants between the spokes alternating golden-leaved herbs like golden marjoram with those that are greenish-blue, like rue, or silvery, like "silver posie" thyme. If you haven't got a real cartwheel to play with, you could lay out pieces of wood to make the same shape. It also looks good using small pieces of rock to form the outer circle. Another idea that works well is to make a wagonwheel shape, on a larger scale, out of small bricks.

WOODEN LADDER

IF YOU have a ladder that is unusable because some of the rungs are unsafe, lay it flat in the garden and use its shape as an edging for the smaller herbs, with the rungs edging their territory. You could cut the ladder in half, of course, and make two matching beds that way, either side of a path. If a conventional ladder is too small-scale for your garden, consider making a ladder-shaped frame for your plants out of bricks. They could either form tiny paths between the herbs, or the whole structure could be raised to make a low ladder-shaped bed, forming the edge of a patio, perhaps.

*An old wagonwheel
makes an effective display
for herbs.*

THYME FOCACCIA

HIS TYPICALLY simple Italian country bread is
traditionally cooked on a stone, or under a mound of
ashes in the hearth. It tastes delicious, especially made
with fresh thyme and black olives.

INGREDIENTS
Makes 1¹/₂-pound
2 cups tepid water
¹/₂ tsp sugar
1 envelope active, dry yeast
6 cups all-purpose flour
2 tsp salt
2 tbs minced thyme
1¹/₂ tbs olive oil
¹/₂ cup black olives, pitted

TIP
**If you can't get
fresh herbs to add
to your homemade
focaccia, dried ones
will do, but add only
half the quantity
shown in the
recipe.**

⬩ Put the tepid water in a bowl and sprinkle
with the sugar and yeast. Leave in a warm place
for about 15 minutes until it starts to froth.
⬩ Mix the flour, salt, and half the thyme together
in a large bowl, then add the oil. Make a hole in
the center and pour in the yeast mix. Stir with a
wooden spoon, gradually taking in the flour
from the sides until thoroughly combined.
Knead into a firm dough that leaves the sides of
the bowl clean.
⬩ Cover the bowl with a damp kitchen towel and
put somewhere warm to double in size.
⬩ Turn the dough out onto a greased baking
sheet and punch it down, spreading it with your
fingers or a flour-dusted rolling pin, to make a
rectangular shape.
⬩ Brush the top with extra olive oil and sprinkle
with the remaining thyme. Poke regular
indentations in the top of the dough and push
olives in them.
Bake in a preheated oven at 450 degrees for
about 35 minutes, or until the top is just turning
golden-brown.

1. *Pour the tepid yeast mixture into the bread mix in the bowl, and stir with a wooden spoon until it makes a dough.*

2. *Make regular indentations in the risen dough with your fingers, and push the olives into them.*

TANSY MAYONNAISE

OU CAN make the basic mayonnaise
in a blender instead of by hand.
Use store-bought mayonnaise if you
prefer as a short cut.

TIP
To make
the classic sauce
tartare, simply add a
tablespoon of lemon
juice and 2 teaspoons
of capers to this
recipe, substituting
1 teaspoon of tarragon
for
the tansy.

INGREDIENTS

1 egg yolk
1 tsp French mustard
½ tsp salt
¼ tsp pepper
1½ tsp sugar
juice of 1 lemon
⅔ cup oil
1 tsp minced young tansy leaves
2 tsp minced parsley

❖ Put the egg yolk in a bowl with the mustard,
salt, pepper, ½ tsp of the sugar, and 1 tsp of the
lemon juice. Mix thoroughly, then beat in the
oil, drop by drop, until the mixture is thick and
smooth. When all the oil has been added, add 3
more teaspoons of lemon juice.

❖ Stir in the tansy, parsley, and remaining sugar.
Mix well, then stir in a further 2 tsp lemon juice.
Serve with egg salad, or fried, broiled or
barbecued fish.

❖ This mayonnaise will keep for several days in
the refrigerator. Strain off the herbs after two or
three days for a less pungent flavor.

TARRAGON PESTO

HE DISTINCTIVE almost aniseed-like flavor of tarragon makes a multitude of accompaniments to serve with meats, cheeses, and eggs. Use tarragon pesto with pasta as a change from the more usual version made with basil.

INGREDIENTS

Serves 4

1/4 cup butter

1 tbs parsley

2 tbs tarragon leaves

2 cloves garlic

3 tbs pinenuts (pignolas) or walnuts

1/2 cup olive oil

1 cup grated Parmesan cheese

❖ Soften the butter (preferably in a microwave oven).
❖ Liquidize the parsley, tarragon, nuts, and garlic with the olive oil in a blender, or grind with a pestle in a mortar.
❖ Stir in the cheese and butter then serve.

TIP
If you find the mixture too overpowering, use the walnuts rather than the pinenuts. Try tarragon for flavoring a dip for crudités, and as a basis for other sauces.

THYME BATH BAGS

TIP
Make up a
strong infusion
of the herbs of
your choice,
strain, and pour
into the
bathwater.

REFRESHING herbal bath can soothe the skin and relax aching muscles, but never fling the herbs straight into the water or they will clog the pipes.

MATERIALS
8-inch square of cheesecloth
dried thyme
raw oatmeal (optional)
twine or tape

⁂ Cut an 8-inch square piece of cheesecloth and place a heap of dried thyme in the center. If you want to soften the water as well, add a little raw oatmeal.

⁂ Gather together the corners and edges of the cheesecloth around the herbs and tie up with a length of tape or twine.

⁂ The bag can be hung from the bath faucet, left to float in the water as the bath fills, or used to scrub the skin.

AROMATIC OVEN GLOVES

VEN GLOVES make practical and attractive presents. Try making them with other mixtures of herbs – mint and marjoram, for instance.

MATERIALS

2 strips patterned fabric 33 × 8 inches
2 pieces matching patterned fabric 8 inches square
2 pieces wadding 8 inches square
7 feet bias binding ¹/₂ inch wide
2 large handfuls dried thyme and tarragon

1. With wrong side up, lay one of the long strips of fabric flat, then place a piece of wadding at each end, matching the raw edges. Tack the wadding in place. With the wrong side facing downward,

place the second long fabric strip over the first and on top of the wadding. Tack the layers of fabric together down the long edges, leaving 8 inches from both sides of each end unstitched. Fold back the top fabric at each end, and place a large handful of dried herbs over both pieces of wadding, spreading the herbs out as evenly as possible.

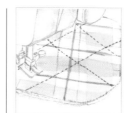

2. Fold the fabric back over the wadding to cover the herbs, and carefully tack through all layers to hold the herbs in place. Cut through all layers of fabric and wadding to round off the 4 corners. Machine or handstitch criss-cross lines over the strip to quilt the fabric.

3. Round off 2 corners of each fabric square to match the long strip. Next, bind along one straight edge of each fabric square with bias binding. Tack a square to each end of the long strip,

matching the raw edges. Tack around the outer edges to form the mitts. To make the loop, fold a 6¹/₂-inch strip of bias binding in half lengthwise and stitch together, folding the raw edges underneath. Fold in half, and tack the loop in place halfway down one side of the oven mitt. Finally, bind along the raw edges of the entire mitt with bias binding to finish. Remove all tacking.

A HERB PRESS

NCE YOU have discovered just how decorative pressed herbs can be, you'll find all sorts of uses for them around the house – try using them to decorate painted furniture, for instance. If you glue them in place, then cover them with five or six layers of varnish, your decoration will last indefinitely. If you are using herbs on any scale you'll need to have a herb press. Make your own – it is quite simple to do.

MATERIALS

2 pieces of 8-inch square plywood
6 8-inch square pieces of card
4 long bolts
4 o-rings
4 wing nuts

1. Drill four holes to take the four bolts just in from the corners of both pieces of plywood, making sure that the holes line up. Diagonally trim the corners of the card.

TIP

If you get the plant pressing bug, make yourself several presses, both small and large, using the same basic technique shown on this page.

2. Assemble the press by pushing the bolts through the plywood, ends upward, from the bottom to the top. Using the washers, screw the top down with the wing nuts, screwing each one down a little in turn so that the plywood does not distort. Put your herbs between the card, placing them between two sheets of tissue then a folded sheet of copy paper.

3. Screw the press down and leave for a day or so, then unscrew to see how your herbs are doing. Paint your press, then decorate with cutout pictures of herbs and flowers. Glue them to the plywood, then give them several coats of acrylic varnish.

THYME, TANSY, AND TARRAGON

INDEX

ACKNOWLEDGMENTS

The publishers would like to thank
the following companies for their help:

BASKETS AND GLASSWARE
Global Village,
Sparrow Works, Bower Hinton, Martock, Somerset.
Telephone: (01935) 823390

DRIED HERBS AND FLOWERS
The Hop Shop,
Castle Farm, Shoreham, Sevenoaks, Kent TN14 7UB.
Telephone: (01959) 523219

HERB PLANTS BY MAIL ORDER
Jekka's Herb Farm,
Rose Cottage, Shellards Lane, Alveston, Bristol BS12 2SY.
Telephone: (01454) 418878

HERB SEEDS
Suffolk Seeds,
Monks Farm, Pantlings Lane, Coggeshall Road,
Kelvedon, Essex CO5 9PG.
Telephone: (01376) 572456

PICTURE CREDITS
Andrew Lawson Photography: pp.35, 86, 133
Photos Horticultural: pp.32, 35TR, BL and BR, 38
Harry Smith Collection: pp.35TL, 112, 124, 129
S & O Matthews Photography: p.83T